I0150581

The Five Approaches to Acting Series

INHABITING THE WORLD OF THE PLAY

WRITTEN BY DAVID KAPLAN

Hansen Publishing Group, LLC
East Brunswick, New Jersey
www.hansenpublishing.com

The Five Approaches to Acting Series: Inhabiting the World of the Play.
Copyright © 2007 David Kaplan

All rights reserved. No part of this book shall be reproduced, stored in a retrieval system, or transmitted by any means, electronic, mechanical, photocopying, recording or otherwise, without written permission from the publisher. No patent liability is assumed with respect to the use of the information contained herein. Although every precaution has been taken in the preparation of this book, the publisher and author assume no responsibility for errors or omissions. Nor is any liability assumed for damages resulting from the use of the information contained herein.

Trademarks

All terms mentioned in this book that are known to be trademarks or service marks have been appropriately capitalized. The publisher and author cannot attest to the accuracy of this information. Use of a term in this book should not be regarded as affecting the validity of any trademark or service mark.

Warning and Disclaimer

Every effort has been made to make this book as complete and as accurate as possible, but no warranty or fitness is implied. The information provided is on an "as is" basis. The author and the publisher shall have neither liability nor responsibility to any person or entity with respect to any loss or damages arising from the information contained in this book.

International Standard Book Number: 978-1-60182-184-3

Hansen Publishing Group, LLC
302 Ryders Lane
East Brunswick, New Jersey
732-220-1211
www.hansenpublishing.com

The Publisher gratefully acknowledges the copyright holders who have agreed to have their works excerpted here. The next page constitutes a continuation of this copyright page.

Excerpts from THE ODD COUPLE copyright © 1966 by Neil Simon, copyright renewed 1994 by Neil Simon. Professionals and amateurs are hereby warned that THE ODD COUPLE is fully protected under the United States Copyright Act, the Berne Convention, and the Universal Copyright Convention and is subject to royalty. All rights, including without limitation professional, amateur, motion picture, television, radio, recitation, lecturing, public reading and foreign translation rights, computer media rights and the right of reproduction, and electronic storage or retrieval, in whole or in part and in any form, are strictly reserved and none of these rights can be exercised or used without written permission from the copyright owner. Inquiries for stock and amateur performances should be addressed to Samuel French, Inc., 45 West 25th Street, New York, NY 10010. All other inquiries should be addressed to Gary N. DaSilva, 111 N. Sepulveda Blvd., Suite 250, Manhattan Beach, CA 90266-6850.
　　Excerpts from THE LEARNED LADIES (THE SCHOOL FOR WIVES) by Jean-Baptiste Poquelin de Molière, English translation copyright © 1978, 1977 by Richard Wilbur, copyright © 1978 by Harcourt, Inc., reprinted by permission of the publisher. CAUTION: Professionals and amateurs are hereby warned that THE LEARNED LADIES is subject to a royalty. It is fully protected under the copyright laws of the United States of America, and of all countries covered by the International Copyright Union (including the Dominion of Canada and the rest of the British Commonwealth), and of all countries covered by the Universal Copyright Convention and the Pan-American Copyright Convention, and of all countries with which the United States has reciprocal copyright relations. All rights, including professional, amateur, motion picture, recitation, lecturing, public reading, radio broadcasting, television and the rights of translation into foreign languages, are strictly reserved. Particular emphasis is laid on the question of readings, permission for which must be secured from the author's agent in writing. All inquiries (except for amateur rights) should be addressed to Gilbert Parker, Curtis Brown Ltd., 575 Madison Avenue, New York NY 10022. The amateur acting rights of THE LEARNED LADIES are controlled exclusively by the Dramatists Play Service, Inc., 440 Park Avenue South, New York, NY 10016. No amateur performances of the play may be given without obtaining in advance the written permission of the Dramatists Play Service Inc., and paying the requisite fee.
　　Excerpts from THE LESSON and THE BALD SOPRANO from *The Bald Soprano and Other Plays* by Eugene Ionesco, translated by Donald M. Allen, © 1958 by Grove Press Inc., used by permission of Grove/Atlantic, Inc.

CREDITS

Excerpts from SOMETIMES I'M HAPPY, by Irving Caesar and Vincent Youmans, copyright © 1925 (Renewed) WB Music Corp. and Irving Caesar Music Corp. All rights Administered by WB Music Corp. All Rights Reserved. Used by Permission. WARNER BROS. PUBLICATIONS U.S. INC., Miami, FL 33014

Excerpts from HEDDA GABLER by Hernrik Ibsen from *The Complete Major Prose Plays of Henrik Ibsen* by Henrik Ibsen, translated by Rolf Fjelde copyright © 1965, 1970, 1978 by Rolf Fjelde. Used by permission of Dutton Signet, a division of Penguin Putnam Inc.

Excerpts from IN THE JUNGLE OF CITIES by Bertolt Brecht, copyright © 1970 by Methuen & Co. Ltd. Reprinted from *In the Jungle of Cities*, reprinted with permission by Arcade Publishing, New York, New York.

Excerpts from THE MAIDS from *The Maids and Deathwatch* by Jean Genet, translated by Bernard Frechtman, copyright © 1954 by Bernard Frechtman, used by permission of Grove/Atlantic, Inc.

Excerpts from LIFE UPON THE WICKED STAGE Words & Music by Jerome Kern and Oscar Hammerstein II © 1927 Universal-PolyGram International Publishing, Inc., a division of Universal Studios, Inc. (ASCAP). Copyright Renewed. International Copyright Secured. All Rights Reserved.

Excerpts from YERMA by Federico Garcia Lorca, translation by James Graham-Lujan and Richard L. O'Connell, from *Three Tragedies*, copyright © 1947 by New Directions Publishing Corp. Reprinted by permission of New Directions Publishing Corp.

Excerpts from the Preface to THE EIFFEL TOWER WEDDING by Jean Cocteau, translation by Dudley Fitts, from *The Infernal Machine and Other Plays*, copyright © 1957 by New Directions Publishing Corp. Reprinted by permission of New Directions Publishing Corp.

Excerpts from DESIRE UNDER THE ELMS from *The Plays of Eugene O'Neill* by Eugene O'Neill, copyright © 1924 and renewed 1952 by Eugene O'Neill. Reprinted by permission of Random House, Inc. CAUTION: Professionals and amateurs are hereby warned that this play, being fully protected under the copyright laws of the United States of America, the British Empire, including the Dominion of Canada, and all other countries of the copyright union, is subject to a royalty. All rights, including professional, amateur, motion pictures, recitation, public reading, radio broadcasting, and the rights of translation into foreign languages are strictly reserved. All inquiries should be addressed to The Dramatists Play Service, Inc., 440 Park Avenue South, New York, NY 10016.

Excerpts from LONG DAY'S JOURNEY INTO NIGHT by Eugene O'Neill, copyright © 1955 by Carlotta Monterey O'Neill. Reprinted by permission of Yale University Press.

Excerpts from THE PERSIANS from *Prometheus Bound and Other Plays* by Aeschylus, translated by Philip Vellacott (Penguin Classics, 1961) copyright © Philip Vellacott, 1961. Reprinted by permission of Penguin Books, Ltd. (UK)

Excerpts from THE GLASS MENAGERIE by Tennessee Williams, copyright © 1945 by University of the South and Edwin D. Williams. Reprinted by permission of New Directions Publishing Corp.

Excerpts from A STREETCAR NAMED DESIRE by Tennessee Williams, copyright © 1947 by University of the South. Reprinted by permission of New Directions Publishing Corp.

Excerpts from BURIED CHILD, copyright © 1979 by Sam Shepard, from *Seven Plays* by Sam Shepard. Used by permission of Bantam Books, a division of Random House, Inc.

Excerpts from ENDGAME by Samuel Beckett, copyright ©1958 by Samuel Beckett; Copyright renewed © 1986 by Samuel Beckett, used by permission of Grove/Atlantic, Inc.

Excerpts from DRUMS IN THE NIGHT by Bertolt Brecht, copyright © 1970 by Methuen & Co. Ltd. Reprinted from *Drums in the Night*, reprinted with permission by Arcade Publishing, New York, New York.

Excerpts from IPHIGENIA IN AULIS reprinted from *Iphigenia in Aulis* by Euripides, translated by Nicholas Rudall, copyright © 1997 by Ivan R. Dee, Inc., translation copyright © 1997 by Nicholas Rudall. By permission of Ivan R. Dee, Publisher.

Excerpts from THE THREE SISTERS from *Chekhov: The Major Plays* by Anton Chekhov, translated by Ann Dunnigan, copyright © 1964 by Ann Dunnigan. Used by permission of Dutton Signet, a division of Penguin Putnam Inc.

Image of Georg Grosz's GETTING THE AXE (DIE RAUEFER) provided by the Print Collection of the Miriam and Ira D. Wallach Division of Art, Prints and Photographs, The New York Public Library, Astor, Lenox, and Tilden Foundations.

Detail from Max Ernst's QUIETUDE provided by the Spencer Collection, The New York Public Library, Astor, Lenox, and Tilden Foundations.

Detail from James Gillray's KING OF BROBDINGNAG AND GULLIVER provided by the Print Collection of the Miriam and Ira D. Wallach Division of Art, Prints and Photographs, The New York Public Library, Astor, Lenox, and Tilden Foundations.

Detail from René Magritte's THE GLASS HOUSE (LA MAISON DE VERRE) permission to reprint provided by copyright © 2001 C. Herscovici/Artists Rights Society (ARS), New York. From the collection and image provided by Museum Boijmans Van Beuningen, Rotterdam.

Detail from René Magritte's CLAIRVOYANCE (LA CLAIRVOYANCE) permission to reprint provided by copyright © 2001 C. Herscovici, Brussels/Artists' Rights Society (ARS), New York. Image provided by Herscovici/Art Resource, NY.

To Edwin W. Schloss,

Prince of friends, open-hearted, open-eyed.

CONTENTS

SCRIPT ANALYSIS COMPARATIVE REFERENCE CHART

	TASK/ACTION ANALYSIS	EPISODIC ANALYSIS	BUILDING IMAGES ANALYSIS	WORLD OF THE PLAY ANALYSIS	NARRATIVE ANALYSIS
BASIC UNIT	Task	Episode	Image	Social context; behavior and form	Event Point of view
ILLUSION OF CHARACTER	Web of relationships	Playing the opposition	String of masks	Distinctions within the context of the world	Intersection of point of view and events
DRAMATIC ACTION	Action meeting an obstacle	Transaction or *gest*	Moment when mask changes	Breach in the rules of the world	Shifting the point of view
KEY QUESTION	What do I need to do?	What do I do? What is my role?	What is this like? What does this make me think of?	What are the values of the world?	What am I describing? What is my point of view?
UNIFYING IMAGE	Oil painting	Poster	Collage	Frame	Film camera angles
RELATIVE THEORY	Freud Psychoanalysis	Alfred Adler Transactional analysis Marxism	Carl Jung Personae	Ruth Benedict Cultural anthropology	Derrida Literary deconstructionism
SUITABLE PLAYWRIGHTS	Chekhov Ibsen Strindberg	Shakespeare Brecht Ionesco	Strindberg Lorca Genet Williams	Molière Wilde O'Neill Beckett	Shakespeare the Greeks Williams Shepard
AUDIENCE	Compassionate	Judgmental	Passionate	Transported	Participatory

PART IV

INHABITING THE WORLD OF THE PLAY

Reading List
Desire Under the Elms by Eugene O'Neill
The Odd Couple by Neil Simon
Patterns of Culture (chapter 8) by Ruth Benedict

James Gillray, detail from *King of Brobdingnag and Gulliver*

CHAPTER 1

COMPARISON

Gulliver's Conclusion

When Lemuel Gulliver—the hero of Jonathan Swift's 1726 novel *Travels into Several Remote Nations of the World*—is shipwrecked on the island of Lilliput, he wakes on the Lilliputian beach surrounded by an army of men six inches tall. Gulliver tries to be considerate under the circumstances, but his tiny hosts consider him gross, dangerous, and loud. Gulliver wins the Lilliputians' confidence only after he butts into their wars, after which they consider him the greatest prodigy ever seen. Granted permission to return to England, Gulliver sails from tiny Lilliput and, shipwrecked once again, lands up on the island of Brobdingnag, where the locals are giants twelve times his size. Although Gulliver acts with dignity with the Brobdingnagians, they hold him in their hands and poke at him like he is a doll. Hiding from a monstrous dog by huddling in a forest of grass blades, Gulliver concludes that ". . . nothing is great or little otherwise than by Comparison."

Is Gulliver big or small? Dainty or gross? It depends on where he is. We could ask similar questions of the plays we've studied so far and reach similar conclusions. Is Hedda Gabler's suicide an act of desperation or triumph? Does Richard III excite or repulse Lady Anne? Does Madame of *The Maids* think she's beautiful or ugly? When the Pupil dies at the end of Ionesco's *Lesson*, is she happy or sad? Answers to these questions can be found by looking at each play as a whole—just as Gulliver was defined by which island he happened to find himself on.

The text of a play is just such an island of meaning and—like tiny Lilliput or gigantic Brobdingnag—a world of its own with its own standards and measures. Like Gulliver, actors inhabiting the world of the play do so in an environment—created or implied by the script—that frames, explains, restricts, amplifies, motivates, and organizes the action of the play and the identity of its characters. A *world of the play analysis* is an investigation of this environment and how it can organize and motivate rehearsals and performance.

The customs of the country

World of the play analysis begins with a strategy for discovering the *rules* of any play. As an actor inhabiting the world of the play, if you understand its rules you'll know who you are, you'll know the meaning of your words and your actions, and, most importantly, you'll know how to survive or fail in that world—and in performance. Think of it as a way to learn the customs of a foreign land you're visiting. You don't have to conform to those customs, of course, but you should know the local laws of etiquette.

Knowing the rules for one play won't help you learn the rules of another. The modest gestures and quiet tones that could make a performance of *Hedda Gabler* believable and effective would have no such effect when used for performances of Lady Anne from *Richard III* or Madame of *The Maids*. Yerma's passion for children has no place in *In the Jungle of Cities*. In order to analyze the world of any play systematically, it helps to look beyond acting techniques to other disciplines—artistic and scientific—that investigate human relationships.

Cultural Anthropology

Seeing a pattern

A good model for world of the play analysis is the social science of *cultural anthropology*. A psychologist might study why you cry at the news of your son's birth; a cultural anthropologist studies why you went to buy cigars and a blue blanket. As an actor inhabiting the world of a play, you should know why you're crying *and* why the blanket is blue. Like actors, cultural anthropologists examine behavior, relationships, emotion, and purpose. And like actors analyzing the world of a play, cultural anthropologists analyze the *context* of behavior, man-made and natural. Predictably harsh winters, for example, might prompt a tribe's trek every autumn to a warmer pasture, establishing a tradition of tent-living. The culture carried along inside those tents would include pots, pans, and prejudices. This culture might reward aggression, punish originality, prize certain colors, or eroticize the sight of a woman's ankles.

The first principle that world of the play analysis borrows from cultural anthropology is *to respect each world, like each culture, separately*. Put into use for actors this means: *The world of the play is its own measure. It isn't gauged by any other.* This is the idea taught by the German-American anthropologist Franz Boas. According to Boas, all aspects of human behavior are relative, without fixed meaning, to be understood and judged in terms of their relationship to the culture as a whole. One culture is not superior to another, neither primitive, barbaric, nor civilized. From one place to another, there is no such thing as "common sense," even when it comes to what would seem like obvious common sense: *don't kill yourself*. As one anthropologist observed:

> We might suppose that in the matter of taking life all peoples would agree in condemnation. On the contrary . . . Suicide may also be a light matter, the recourse of anyone who has suffered some slight rebuff, an act that occurs constantly in a tribe. It may be the highest and noblest act a wise man can perform. The very tale of it, on the other hand, may be a matter of incredulous mirth, and the act itself impossible to conceive as a human possibility. Or it may be a crime punishable by law, or regarded as a sin against the gods (66).

This insight can point the way to an actor's interpretation. Hedda Gabler's suicide should be evaluated within the world of the play; it shouldn't be judged according to its value in our world, or even Ibsen's. Hedda kills herself in a world where painful endurance—no matter what—is an expected way of life. When the last character who speaks (a judge, significantly) hears that Hedda has killed herself, he says, "People don't do such things." Hedda's offstage pistol shot is her last defiance of what is expected from her. Suicide within the world of *Hedda Gabler* can be considered an act of strength, not weakness (although there are other interpretations, of course). In the pitiless world of Brecht's *In the Jungle of Cities*, survival at any cost is the highest good; suicide, for whatever reason, would be an act of failure and defeat. These may or may not be the values of the audience members, or the playwright, or even of the onstage characters. They are the values of the world in which the play takes place.

Ruth Benedict's Model

That quote about suicide was written by a student of Franz Boas—a quiet, shy woman who always wore the same dress for class when she was Boas's teaching assistant at Barnard College. On those occasions when she had to speak to the class on her own, she was often awkward, but as one of her later students described: "between the 'uh' and 'ah' often came a bombshell of light which changed everything" (67). Her name was Ruth Benedict, and she theorized that each culture had a central idea that organized that culture like a "personality writ large." This is the second theory of cultural anthropology to adapt for use in an actor's analysis of a play: *the rules of the play make a pattern*.

When one value is held highest, others are less important by comparison, and this configuration adds up to the characteristics of a consistent world. In Shakespeare's *Richard III*, pity and scruples are not as important as self-conviction and aggression. A deformed hunchback double-crosses his allies, arranges the murder of his brother and best friends, orders the death of children, and seduces the widow of a man he has killed. In our world, Richard is a wretch; in his own world he is the King. When playing such a role, it doesn't help to condemn Richard or even to investigate his motives; it helps to understand him in the context of the world in which he is set.

Ruth Benedict's theory offers an actor a good understanding of how such a wretch could become King. Her first and most influential book, *Patterns of Culture* (1934), summarized years of research, thinking, and comparative analysis. Boas, by the way, wrote the introduction. For each of the cultures she examined, Benedict claimed to have identified a pattern that influenced the way tribe members perceived and lived in the world. Individuals, of course, rebelled or fit in, but they all measured themselves by the local standards, and within the accepted pattern. Like the physical dimensions of Gulliver's hosts, this cultural pattern or configuration determined identity and meaning.

Benedict's first field studies were among the Zuni communities of the American southwest, a people who valued sobriety and inoffensiveness above all other virtues. They disliked charisma. If he had been born in a Zuni pueblo, someone like Richard III would have been hung by his thumbs as a witch. Five years later, Benedict was startled to find that the Pima Indians—near neighbors of the Zuni who lived in the same desert conditions—thought that conflict and ecstasy were the essence of existence. Had someone like Richard III lived among *them*, where fighting was the highest of virtues, he would have thrived (although he probably would have been despised for his relentless opportunism).

In organizing her field research, Benedict did not rank the two tribes as better or worse, but respected them as systems of their own. She labeled them as *Dionysian* and *Apollonian*, based on which value the group held highest: ecstasy or calm. These labels were borrowed from an essay about Greek tragedy by the German philosopher Friedrich Nietzsche. Later, Benedict added a dour group of South Pacific Islanders—called the Dobu—as a third example of a psychological frame of mind, which she called *paranoid*. Richard III would have been quite at home among the Dobu. Benedict writes:

> The motivations that run through all Dobuan existence are singularly limited . . . All existence is cut-throat competition, and every advantage is gained at the expense of a defeated rival . . . The good man, the successful man, is he who has cheated another of his place (68).

In the pattern of Richard III's world, a ruthless man is characteristic and admirable, just as in the Dobu's world. Richard's butchery is therefore exemplary, not monstrous. This is the third principle to be taken from cultural anthropology: *A role should be characterized within the context of the play*. In Brecht's *In the Jungle of Cities*, savagery is normal, reticence a disease. Garga's mildness would be praised among the Zuni. But among the Dobu, Garga, like all people "of sunny, kindly disposition who like work and like to be helpful," would be considered "silly and simple and definitely crazy" (69).

Even before *Patterns of Culture* was published, Benedict wrote an article for the *Journal of General Psychology* that urged psychologists and psychiatrists to encourage tolerance for less-usual types in our own culture, since ideas of normal and abnormal were relative. In 1937, Karen Horney, an American psychoanalyst directly influenced by Benedict, also challenged the accepted theories of psychology to redefine "normal" and "abnormal" as particular to culture. According to Horney (who wished her name to be pronounced *Horn-eye*), there was no one biologically inevitable psychology—as Freud had claimed. There was, for example, no inevitable women's envy of men, there was no inevitable rivalry with one's father. These were the definitions of the society in which Freud lived, where men were powerful, women were not, and winning a competition was the goal of life. In a society where women were powerful, there would be and was envy of men for women. In a society that endorsed compromise, fathers and sons would have less competitive relations.

Horney's acceptance of Benedict's theory of a culture as "a personality writ large" was and is unusual. Among most other scientists, Benedict's theory is controversial. Her labels "Dionysian" and "Apollonian" are subjective and interpretive, by definition unscientific. Like stereotypes, they reduce complex and dynamic forces to a single word: *serene, ecstatic,* or *paranoid*. Another complaint is that Benedict did not sufficiently take into account that cultural patterns are always changing, and a cultural environment rarely, if ever, has clear origins or borders. Yet the criticisms of Benedict's theory as science reinforce its perhaps more appropriate application to the analysis of the world of a play. A play *is* finite in time and space: it begins and ends. Its borders are marked by a curtain or a raised platform or a line drawn on the ground. It has a limited number of people to compare. Its sources are generally known, and the subjectivity of an organizing image like *Dionysian* or *ecstatic* is exactly what an actor is looking for to galvanize his performance.

Significantly, Ruth Benedict was partially deaf, and grew deafer as she grew older. Like Stanislavsky watching Duse perform in Italian, or Brecht watching Mei Lanfang perform in Chinese, wherever Benedict went she paid close attention to what her subjects did, separately from her grasp of what they were saying. Her built-in deference to the foreign culture being observed set up a habit of observation that was antithetical to the aloof and distanced protocol of other researchers. In order to read lips, she needed, like an actor, to understand the *emotional images* of the speaker with whom she was trying to communicate.

Reading Shakespeare in context

The similarity of Ruth Benedict's methods to an actor's is not a coincidence. In 1946, two years before she died, in her last speech as President of the American Anthropology Association, Benedict revealed that her insight of how meaning changes from culture to culture had been shaped by reading Shakespeare criticism. The texts written by Shakespeare, she explained, had been known and performed for four centuries; from her own reading of each era's critics she had learned how each era read very different meanings into the same words. Criticism, she wrote, also taught techniques for studying symbols and arranging what seemed like a writer's free associations into patterns (70).

At the same time Benedict was reading Shakespeare criticism and organizing *Patterns of Culture*, critics of Shakespeare were lining up new systems of criticism that closely paralleled Benedict's ideas. In 1930, the British critic G. Wilson Knight laid out the new guidelines in *On the Principles of Shakespeare Interpretation*:

1. We should first regard each play as a visionary unit bound to obey none but its own self-imposed laws.
2. [We should] . . . relate any given incident or speech either to the time-sequence of the story or the peculiar atmosphere, intellectual or imaginative, which binds the play. . . . we should not look for perfect verisimilitude to life, but rather see each play as an expanded metaphor . . . It will then usually appear that many difficult actions and events become coherent and with the scope of their universe, natural (71).

Following G. Wilson Knight's lead, a very influential essay with the sarcastic title "How Many Children Had Lady Macbeth?" was published in 1933 by another British critic, L.C. Knights. Knights considered any modern search for a Shakespearean character's motivation as further evidence of a reluctance to master the words of the play—as inadequate a method for explaining the meaning of these roles as the Victorian era's sentimental biographies that invented answers to the essay's title question. Knights declared that Shakespeare's texts only made sense when one started with "so many lines of verse on a printed page. . . ." The key to understanding the plays, Knights wrote, was "the unique arrangement of words that constitutes these plays" (72).

For example, in Chapter 7 it was pointed out that when clothing is mentioned in *Macbeth*, it is associated with an image of clothing borrowed—or stolen—from someone else. Other associations in *Macbeth* cluster around this same idea of false or unnatural appearance. The play begins with witches described as women who have men's beards. "Fair is foul," they say at the end of the first short scene. Macbeth, too, announces as he enters, "So fair and foul a day I have not seen."

Similar images throughout the five acts of *Macbeth* build what Shakespeare critics called a *recurring theme* of the play: unnatural nature, named within the play itself as *equivocation*, a lie passed off as the truth. If she had observed this in a field study, Ruth Benedict would have called this recurring pattern the "personality writ large."

An actor answering the question *Is Macbeth a bad man or a good man?* should do so in the context of the play. Within the world of equivocation, Macbeth can be understood to have equivocal motivations and obstacles. The smiling traitor, the trusted nobleman who kills his King—like a woman with a beard or a day simultaneously fair and foul—Macbeth is a living mix of opposites: a good man who does bad things.

Meaning in the world of *Macbeth* also depends on the form in which the characters speak. Here, as in the other plays written in iambic pentameter by Shakespeare, "natural" speech is poetry with ten syllables to a line. Ten-syllable lines tap out a base rhythm, as in the unsuspecting King's appreciation of the place where he is to be killed:

> This / cas / tle / hath / a / plea / sant / seat; / the / air (10)
> Nim / bly / and / sweet / ly / re / com / mends / it / self (10)

Set against a norm of ten syllables, deviations of fewer and more syllables are significant, and often characterize the speaker as disturbed in some way—even a harmonious character like Ross, here describing the King's murder:

> Thou / seest / the / hea / vens, / as / troubl / ed / with / man's / act, (11)
> Threat / en / his / blood / y / stage: / by / the / clock / tis / day, (11)
> And / yet / dark / night / strang / les / the / trav / el / ing / lamp. (11)

The lines are overloaded with syllables because the speaker is overcharged with emotion. Among plays by Shakespeare, *Macbeth*, with its central theme of distortion, is one of the texts with the most frequent distortion of the verse pattern: many lines of nine, eleven, twelve, and thirteen. Audience members are not tapping out the number of syllables with their feet, but the repetition, like the beat of music, sets up a visceral response when the "normal" rhythm is broken. Anything an actor might try is set within this rhythm and variation. An actor concentrating on inner imagery to the exclusion of such technical considerations will sabotage the possible effect of psychological motives or motivated behavior.

Read according to Knight and Knights, the text called *The Tragedy of Macbeth* is its own unique system of meaning. That system is made up of words that are configured around recurring themes. The character called Macbeth, or any character in the play, can only be understood against the grid of those words. From criticism or from anthropology, then, we can borrow similar concepts to define the world of the play.

Terms to Work with: The Rules of the World of the Play

The world of the play

The **world of the play** includes the specific environments within which the play is set and performed, the form in which the play is written, and the rules that measure the behavior of characters set within the world. World of the play analysis considers the play as a whole. If you want to approach your work with a world of the play analysis, it helps to look at all the scenes of the play, not just the ones you are in. Look at all the roles, not just your own. Only when the rules for the play are understood can a role, specific behavior, or episode be understood.

Other disciplines use different terms to describe a similar idea: in psychology, the word is *gestalt* (from the German word meaning "configuration"); in anthropology, the words used in place of Ruth Benedict's *pattern* can be *cultural configuration* or a *culture* among other cultures. Besides being simpler, the word *world* has a history that recommends its use—which has nothing to do with land or territory. *World* comes from the language called Old German, and is made up of two words: *wer*, meaning "man" (as in "werewolf"!), and *ald*, as in "age" or "time." Literally *wer-ald* mean "man time" or "era." In literature it is called the *worldview* or, as in the title of E.M.W. Tillyard's excellent book: *The Elizabethan World Picture*. As we have in other chapters, let's agree to call the idea by the same name and move on.

Also, as in other chapters, the world of the play is an interpretation. Barren, Yerma can be seen as pathetic in a world where women are meant to have children. Barren, Yerma can be seen as a heroine in a world where women are meant to have children, so strong in her purpose that she is willing to kill what stands in her way. There is no single interpretation, although there are useful ways to look for answers in order to establish a set of *rules*.

The rules and patterns of the world of the play

The **rules** of the world of the play organize the behavior and the environment in that world. The rules do not govern, they are a measure. Not everyone conforms. A big mistake—and a common one—is to think that every character you play is wise, beautiful, strong, and a winner. No. World of the play analysis allows you to measure your character against other characters and to define weakness or strength in an active relationship with other characters. Not everyone is as beautiful as you are, or as intelligent—but then again, your intelligence might count for nothing in the world, just as Gulliver's didn't when the King of Brobdingnag picked him up and examined him like an insect.

Once you define the rules of the world of the play, you can identify a **pattern** of behavior governed by those rules. The pattern is the consistent configuration of behavior in the play; it is the context, the system of meaning within which roles are characterized. World of the play analysis identifies and collects details of behavior and dialogue in order to relate them to deeper patterns embedded in the text.

The Ten Questions

How can you begin defining the rules of the world so that you can begin to identify the play's patterns? The rules of the world are derived, at first, from the answers to **ten questions**. You can, should, and will ask more questions than ten. You can refine and clarify your vision by adding three more questions at every rehearsal and performance, but, to begin, answer at least these ten. They need not be asked in this sequence. If you want, you can notice that the questions are in categories that correspond to anthropological study. You don't have to notice that. Just answer the questions.

Here are the ten questions with quick answers—all of them interpretations, not absolutes—from the scenes we've already analyzed for tasks, episodes, and images.

- **In the world of this play, what is beautiful and what is ugly?**
  In the world of *Hedda Gabler*, traditions are beautiful, innovations are ugly. In the world of *The Maids*, artifice is beautiful, to be plain and unadorned is to be ugly.
- **In the world of this play, what is strong and what is weak?**
  In the world of *Richard III*, sureness of purpose is strong, doubt is weak. In the world of *Yerma*, instinct is strong, the rules of society are weak.
- **In the world of this play, what is wisdom and what is ignorance?**
  In the world of *In the Jungle of Cities*, knowing how to undermine your rival is wisdom, ignorance is believing in compromise. In the world of *The Maids*, wisdom is understanding that reality is a manufactured façade, ignorance is accepting things for what they seem to be.
- **In the world of this play, what is skill and what is ineptitude?**
  In *In the Jungle of Cites*, cunning is a skill, compassion is ineptitude. In *The Maids*, skill is the ability to tell a convincing lie; when you get caught lying you're inept. (Notice that wisdom and ignorance are states of mind, skill and ineptitude are things you do.)
- **In the world of this play, what is common and what is elite?**
  In the world of *Richard III*, civilians are common, warriors are elite. In the world of *The Lesson*, Pupils are common, Professors are elite.
- **In the world of this play, what is polite and what is not polite?**
  In the world of *The Lesson*, it is polite for the Pupil to obey the Professor. It is not polite to be too smart. In the world of *Hedda Gabler*, it is polite to suffer in silence. It is not polite to shoot yourself dead. (Notice that the difference between polite and elite is that polite depends on *what you do*, elite is *who you are*.)

- **In the world of this play, what is good and what is evil?**
  In the world of *Yerma*, it is good to have a child, it is evil to be barren. In the world of *Hedda Gabler*, convention is good, eccentricity is evil.
- **In the world of this play, how do people survive?**
  In the world of *Richard III*, people survive by lying, deceiving, outwitting, and back-stabbing. In the world of *Hedda Gabler*, people survive by hard work, narrow vision, and aping conventional morals. Hedda does not survive, but her husband and her friend live after her.
- **In the world of this play, how do people improve?**
  In the world of *The Lesson*, the Pupil improves by obeying the Professor—even if that means dying. In the world of *Richard III*, people improve by killing their rivals.
- **In the world of this play, how do people win or lose?**
  In the world of *Yerma*, you win by having a baby. This is not a world of adoption, abortion, or planned parenting. In the world of *The Maids*, people win when they meld illusion with reality. In *The Maids*, people lose when they're stuck with their plain, banal lives. In the anti-romantic *In the Jungle of Cities*, you lose if you fall in love.

There will be some overlap and repetition in answering the ten questions, but not as much as you would think. In some worlds, strong is not beautiful (*Richard III*), polite is not elite (*In the Jungle of Cities*), and skill is not wisdom (*Yerma*). Notice that for Hedda the world is ugly; for her husband George and his Aunt Juju, it is beautiful. George, who has a conventional mind, is a survivor; Hedda, who embraces originality, is doomed. Richard III is ruthless, a virtue in his world; his prey, Lady Anne, for all her "virtues" in other worlds, lacks common sense in this one.

Notice also that answering the ten questions helps direct and define the results of previous approaches already used to investigate scenes. The glamorous image Madame has of herself is foolish and self-deluding. Out of her finery, Madame is as common and as ugly as her maids, although she doesn't know it. The episode of Richard seducing Anne is reinterpreted as theft: on his way to steal the throne, Richard steals a dead man's wife. Hedda's motivation is revealed as defiance, and her flirtation with Mr. Løvborg is motivated by rebellion against society, rather than sexual attraction.

Finding Answers to the Ten Questions: Analyzing *Desire Under the Elms*

Let's answer the ten questions in our analysis of a scene from Eugene O'Neill's 1924 *Desire Under the Elms* (73) and see how the behavior in the scene can then be interpreted. Later, we'll look at ways that this scene can help with the interpretation of other scenes in the play, and how knowing the rules of the world of the play will structure rehearsals.

Eugene O'Neill was the first American to receive a Nobel Prize for literature. He based the text of *Desire Under the Elms* on an ancient Greek myth—the story of Phaedra's unrestrained love for her stepson Hippolytus. The same subject was already the source for two other famous plays: *Hippolytus* written by Euripides in 428 BCE in Greek verse and *Phèdre*, written in 1677 by Jean Racine, who set the story in rhyming twelve-syllable French couplets, called *alexandrines*. O'Neill set his American stepson/stepmother love story in Vermont in 1850. The play is written in a rural New England dialect, which makes it difficult to read. It makes it difficult to translate, too, but that hasn't stopped the play from taking its place in the world repertory. In 1999, there was a production in Belgrade; in the 1980s it was performed in Mongolia. There have been productions in Russia since the 1920s.

This excerpt is from the fourth scene of the first act. The stepmother has yet to enter. The section we'll look at begins with two characters O'Neill added to the story, Simeon and Peter, two other sons from the father's previous marriage.

> SIMEON *and* PETER *stare at the sky with a numbed appreciation.*

PETER Purty!

SIMEON Ay-eh. Gold's t' the East now.

PETER Sun's startin' with us fur the Golden West.

SIMEON (*staring around the farm, his compressed face tightened, unable to conceal his emotion*) Waal—it's our last mornin'—mebbe.

PETER (*the same*) Ay-eh.

SIMEON (*stamps his foot on the earth and addresses it desperately*) Waal—ye've thirty year o' me buried in ye—spread out over ye—blood an' bone an' sweat—rotted away—fertilizin' ye—richin' yer soul—prime manure, by God, that's what I been t'ye!

PETER Ay-eh! An' me!

SIMEON An' yew, Peter. (*he sighs—then spits*) Waal—no use'n cryin' over spilt milk.

PETER They's gold in the West—an' freedom mebbe. We been slaves t' stone walls here.

SIMEON (*defiantly*) We hain't nobody's slaves from this out—nor no thin's slaves nuther. (*a pause—restlessly*) Speakin' o' milk, wonder how Eben's managin'?

The play itself will define its world—and in direct words

When spoken aloud and acted onstage, the words of the text set out the rules that govern the world of the play. Often, those rules are established directly. A character will announce that *this is beautiful, this is strong*, and *this is my idea of good.*

- "Fair is foul and foul is fair," say the witches in *Macbeth*, and they're not kidding.
- "It's better to know which is more important, a pound of fish or an opinion," Shlink announces in *In the Jungle of Cities*.
- "People don't do such things," says the Judge at the end of *Hedda Gabler*.

COMPARISON

In this scene from *Desire Under the Elms*, some statements are made:

- The sky is pretty.
- People are manure to the earth.
- There's no use crying over spilt milk.

From this, it's not too complicated to begin to answer some of our questions:

- In the world of *Desire Under the Elms*, the sky and the earth are beautiful. Men are not beautiful, they are manure.
- In the world of *Desire Under the Elms*, it is polite to conserve your emotions: compress them, numb them, control them. It is rude to waste them.

Although these statements are made by individual characters, they hold true for the entire play. Similar statements are made in earlier scenes as well as in later scenes.

The historical period and setting help establish the rules

Although he was writing in 1924, O'Neill set his play in 1850, in New England. Life in that place at that time was tied to the land. The soil was rocky, difficult to farm, and yielded few rewards. Labor was hard and unforgiving. There were few emotional outlets. Church-going was orderly and dull, New England churches no longer the places of ecstasy or torment they had been a hundred years earlier.

In 1848, far from the Atlantic coast, gold was discovered out West, free for the panning out of California's rivers. The chance to strike it rich was a direct challenge to the Puritan work ethic, an alternative to hand-to-mouth subsistence picking rocks out of the Connecticut soil. Going to California meant abandoning life as it was known: those who chose to stay East accepted a life of hardship.

Also, in 1850 the argument over slavery was building to the Civil War, which would erupt a decade later. It was a point of pride with New Englanders that they were free men, not slaves, who owned the land they worked. This pride in possession compensated for their back-breaking work. Peter and Simeon realize that they'll never own the farm they've been working, so they're leaving New England. Eben, the third son (in the role of Hippolytus), is happy to do both his and his brothers' chores; he thinks of the farm as his eventual inheritance. His stepmother Abbie (in the Phaedra role) will explain that she married Eben's father, Ephraim, so she wouldn't have to work for someone else. In other plays—and worlds—working for someone else is not the horror it is made out to be here. With these ideas in mind, a few more questions can be answered:

- In the world of this play, it's bad to be owned by someone; it's good to be free.
- In the world of this play, there's freedom in the West. The play takes place in the East, by inference the land of servitude.

  PETER They's gold in the West—an' freedom mebbe. We been slaves t' stone walls here.

SIMEON (*defiantly*) We hain't nobody's slaves from this out—nor no thin's slaves nuther. (*a pause—restlessly*) Speakin' o' milk, wonder how Eben's managin'?

PETER I s'pose he's managin'.

SIMEON Mebbe we'd ought t'help—this once.

PETER Mebbe. The cows knows us.

SIMEON An' likes us. They don't know him much.

PETER An' the hosses, an' pigs, an' chickens. They don't know him much.

SIMEON They knows us like brothers—an' likes us! (*proudly*) Hain't we raised 'em t' be fust-rate, number one prize stock?

PETER We hain't—not no more.

SIMEON (*dully*) I was fergittin'. (*then resignedly*) Waal, let's go help Eben a spell an' git waked up.

PETER Suits me.

They are starting off down left, rear, for the barn when EBEN *appears from there, hurrying toward them, his face excited.*

Notice that the rules of the world are established not only from what the characters say, but also from what they do—their behavior. From these lines and the behavior associated with them, we learn more:

- In the world of this play, people survive by doing their chores and by serving a hard master.
- In the world of this play, it is impossible to win. You can only escape.

Understand that the historical period is a rendering of the playwright's—what the writer understands and what the writer selects to include in the action of the play. O'Neill's 1850s America is his own creation, like Shakespeare's Rome or Brecht's Chicago, and not a historical reality. In 1850, not too far from the setting of this play, Herman Melville wrote home to his friends in New York that he was finishing *Moby Dick* on sweet Berkshire grass. The New England grass is certainly not sweet in *Desire Under the Elms*.

The time and place in which the play was written help to establish the rules

The environment in which the play was written is often more important for a world of the play analysis than the period in which the play is set. Think of the different versions of "Cleopatra." Bernard Shaw's witty Egypt defines a very different Cleopatra from Shakespeare's romantic Egypt. Claudette Colbert's Cleopatra and Elizabeth Taylor's and Sarah Bernhardt's are all very different too, reflections of the fashions in the world that created them. Think of Liz and Dick's 1960s *La Dolce Vita* version or Colbert's 1932 soigné evening gowns and Art Deco cruise on Cecil B. DeMille's glassy Nile.

COMPARISON

When *Desire Under the Elms* was written in 1924, traditional American values were as challenged as they had been in the 1850s. During the 1920s, American women voted for the first time. Sexuality was more openly expressed, especially in popular dance and in the movies, where a new female character, the "vamp" (short for vampire), modernized the late-nineteenth century's fear that a woman's sexuality would steal a man's power.*

The most significant challenge to America's traditional values was the new popular science of psychology: Sigmund Freud's theory that behavior was a function of sexual desire, especially repressed desire. Because Freud's theories explained the dynamic of American repression and predicted its inevitable end, they appealed especially to American intellectuals. *The old God is dead*, wrote O'Neill, *and what can take his place?* The answer for many people was the psychology identified by Freud as universal, among them the daughter's inevitable desire for her father and hatred of her mother, called the *Electra complex*. The *Oedipus complex* was Freud's theory of a similarly inevitable competition between father and son for the mother's love.

These complexes resonated with many Americans as explanations for the conflict between generations and changing social patterns. O'Neill used the Electra complex for his 1932 retelling of Greek myth in American images, *Mourning Becomes Electra*. In *Desire Under the Elms*, he added the Oedipus complex to the ancient story of Phaedra and Hippolytus and insisted on a motivation not to be found in the original: that the stepson was consciously stealing the stepmother from the father.

SIMEON Waal, let's go help Eben a spell an' git waked up.
PETER Suits me.

> *They are starting off down left, rear, for the barn when* EBEN *appears from there, hurrying toward them, his face excited.*

EBEN (*breathlessly*) Waal—har they be! The old mule an' the bride! I seen 'em from the barn down below at the turnin'.
PETER How could ye tell that far?
EBEN Hain't I as far-sight as he's near-sight? Don't I know the mare an' buggy, an' two people settin' in it? Who else . . .? An' I tell ye I kin feel 'em a-comin', too! (*he squirms as if he had an itch*)
PETER (*beginning to be angry*) Waal—let him do his own unhitchin'!
SIMEON (*angry in his turn*) Let's hustle in an' git our bundles an' be a-going' as he's a-comin'. I don't want never t'step inside the door agen arter he's back. (*They both start back around the corner of the house.* EBEN *follows them*)
EBEN (*anxiously*) Will ye sign it afore ye go?
PETER Let's see the color o' the old skinflint's money an' we'll sign.

---

*You can see vamps flouncing about in *Orphans of the Storm*. They're the lascivious party girls with black rings of make-up around their eyes that give them the appearance of raccoons. Not a bad image for Madame in *The Maids*.

They disappear left. The two brothers clump upstairs to get their bundles. EBEN *appears in the kitchen, runs to the window, peers out, comes back and pulls up a strip of flooring in under stove, takes out a canvas bag and puts it on the table, then sets the floorboard back in place. The two brothers appear a moment after. They carry old carpetbags.*

Another change in American society in the 1920s that O'Neill was sensitive to was the redefinition of American values into increasingly material terms. The Protestant idea that God rewards hard work was harnessed by the growing and persuasive field of advertising to convince the public that the accumulation of bought and sold objects could improve a person's soul. "The business of America is business," said Calvin Coolidge, the taciturn American president at the time (who, not coincidentally, was from New England). O'Neill wrote that it disgusted him to think that the progress of the human race was now to be measured by the acquisition of material goods.

EBEN (*puts his hand on bag guardingly*) Have ye signed?

SIMEON (*shows paper in his hand*) Ay-eh. (*greedily*) Be that the money?

EBEN (*opens bag and pours out pile of twenty-dollar gold pieces*) Twenty-dollar pieces—thirty of 'em. Count 'em. (PETER *does so, arranging them in stacks of five, biting one or two to test them*)

PETER Six hundred. (*he puts them in bag and puts it inside his shirt carefully*)

SIMEON (*handing paper to* EBEN) Har ye be.

EBEN (*after a glance, folds it carefully and hides it under his shirt—gratefully*) Thank yew.

PETER Thank yew for the ride.

SIMEON We'll send ye a lump o' gold fur Christmas. (*A pause.* EBEN *stares at them and they at him*)

PETER (*awkwardly*) Waal—we're a-goin'.

SIMEON Coming out t' the yard?

EBEN No. I'm waitin' in here a spell.

Another silence. The brothers edge awkwardly to door in rear—then turn and stand.

SIMEON Waal—good-by.

PETER Good-by.

The bag of gold is a prop from a melodrama and is meant to be misleading. In the world of this play, people do not get rich or improve their lives with money. The characters *think* they improve by accumulating wealth, but by the play's end they learn that none of that has worth. In the last scene, Ephraim Cabot, the father, claims that he too will go to California, but the gold he saved to pay for such a trip is gone and he is forced to live his life in the hard way God wants him to.

- In the world of this play, it is common to work the soil, to pay attention to traditional values. It is elite to ignore them.
- In the world of this play, it is skill to squeeze money out of rocks. It is inept to give money away or let it be stolen.

The author's value system

Sometimes a playwright will organize the world of a play with his own systematic insight into life. Some playwrights really worked at their systems like philosophers. You may recall from Chapter 7 that the Swedish playwright August Strindberg held the belief that the world was organized into vampires and their victims. So when you're acting in a play by Strindberg, it's good to ask: *Am I the vampire or the victim? Do I survive by sucking the life force out of people around me, or am I the person who is being drained?* Strindberg also believed that there was an ongoing war between the sexes. He further held that women naturally bonded against men and met in secret to discuss strategy. Now, whether it's true or not isn't the point. Strindberg wasn't creating a mirror, he was creating an energy-charged world of his own imagination that, yes, did have some relationship to corseted nineteenth-century Scandinavian sex roles.

Similarly, the American playwright Tennessee Williams created an imaginary landscape inhabited by noble losers and virile survivors. It helps to know that, to Williams, losing was noble, not shameful. It's equally useful when playing the murderous *Maids* to know that being a criminal was glamorous to their creator, Jean Genet.

Of necessity, a playwright has a vision of the world as relationships between people, and often a playwright will have a vision that he has developed from play to play. That doesn't mean that all of a playwright's plays have the same value systems, but some playwrights seem to be visiting the same imaginary world repeatedly. In the many plays O'Neill wrote within the decade, his return to the structure of a Freudian pattern is consistent, especially his dramatic use of tension between public behavior and the unexpressed subconscious. In *Desire Under the Elms*, as in his other plays, a system of values is set out directly by statements and stage action. Here is O'Neill's description of Ephraim Cabot's abandon during a square dance from later in the play:

> CABOT (. . . *suddenly, unable to restrain himself any longer, he prances into the midst of the dancers, scattering them, waving his arms about wildly*) Ye're all hoofs! Git out o' my road! Give me room! I'll show ye dancin'. Ye're all too soft! (*He pushes them roughly away. They crowd back toward the walls, muttering, looking at him resentfully*)
>
> FIDDLER (*jeeringly*) Go it, Ephraim! Go it.
>
> *He starts "Pop, Goes the Weasel," increasing the tempo with every verse until at the end he is fiddling crazily as fast as he can go.* CABOT *starts to dance, which*

he does very well and with tremendous vigor. Then he begins to improvise, cuts incredibly grotesque capers, leaping up and cracking his heels together, prancing around in a circle with body bent in an Indian war dance, then suddenly straightening up and kicking as high as he can with both legs. He is like a monkey on a string. And all the while he intersperses his antics with shouts and derisive comments.

CABOT Whoop! Here's dancin' fur ye! Whoop! See that! Seventy-six, if I'm a day! Hard as iron yet! . . .

The undeniable effect of this onstage is the establishment of another rule: *In the world of this play, under a veneer, the savage power of the body is strong. Civilization is weak.*

Acknowledged or not, an author's insight is affected by the circumstances of his life, and it's useful to know those circumstance when determining the rules of the play. Be careful here. In defining the author's value system, it is a mistake to interpret the play as a symptom of the playwright's life. However, if we examine *Desire Under the Elms*, Eugene O'Neill's personal life does organize this play—and every other play he ever wrote that contained father and son characters.

EBEN Good-by.

They go out. He sits down at the table, faces the stove and pulls out the paper. He looks from it to the stove. His face, lighted up by the shaft of sunlight from the window, has an expression of trance. His lips move. The two brothers come out to the gate.

PETER (*looking off toward barn*) Thar he be—unhitchin'.

SIMEON (*with a chuckle*) I'll bet ye he's riled!

PETER An thar she be.

SIMEON Let's wait'n'see what our new Maw looks like.

PETER (*with a grin*) An' give him our partin' cuss!

SIMEON (*grinning*) I feel like raisin' fun. I feel light in my head an' feet.

PETER Me, too. I feel like laffin' till I'd split up the middle.

SIMEON Reckon it's the likker?

PETER No. My feet feel itchin' t'walk an' walk—an' jump high over thin's—an'. . .

SIMEON Dance? (*a pause*)

PETER (*puzzled*) It's plumb onnateral.

SIMEON (*a light coming over his face*) I calc'late it's 'cause school's out. It's holiday. Fur once we're free!

PETER (*dazedly*) Free?

COMPARISON

In life, O'Neill's father was the actor James O'Neill, who began his career with the potential to become a master of classical roles, but out of constant fear of poverty limited himself to repeating the same successful swashbuckling role from the melodramatic play based on the Dumas novel *The Count of Monte Cristo*. O'Neill's mother was a soft person and a drug addict, easily swayed by her stingy husband. O'Neill blamed his father for his mother's drug addiction, and rebelled against his family by running off to sea as a sailor. Wraith-like mothers are part of the O'Neill mythology. So are skin-flint fathers associated with the word "stinking"—a combination unforgettable to anyone who knows O'Neill's masterpiece *Long Day's Journey into Night* (published 1956), a play with two sons, a wraith-like mother, and a stingy father.

"You stinking old miser!" The younger son Jamie, who has tuberculosis, hurls these words at his father, who is deciding whether to send Jamie to a cheap state-run sanatorium. "To think when it's a question of your son having consumption, you can show yourself up before the whole town as such a stinking old tightwad!" (74). *Long Day's Journey* is a family saga so frankly autobiographical that O'Neill wrote the play with tears streaming down his face.

> JAMIE (*trying to control his sobs*) I've known about Mama so much longer than you. Never forget the first time I got wise. Caught her in the act with a hypo. Christ, I'd never dreamed before that any women but whores took dope! (74)

Defying one's father and then *cursing one's father* are major actions in the world of *Desire Under the Elms*, or any O'Neill play. The playwright spent his whole life writing about these subjects, setting them in worlds where:

- It is skill to be hard, it is inept to be soft.
- Mothers are soft, fathers are hard.
- Freedom is so rare it is practically unimaginable.

O'Neill's ideas are specific to his life. In playing a son or father or mother in one of his plays, it is important to understand that these family roles make up a system, like a mythology. Your memories of your own father are probably not those of Eugene O'Neill's. For O'Neill, the pride of a father is that of possession, not love. It is promiscuously sentimental to work yourself up about dear old dad until you first understand what it means to be a dad in the world of the play.*

---

*Ruth Benedict has something pertinent to say about this in *Patterns of Culture*: "Without the clue that in our civilization at large man's paramount aim is to amass private possessions and multiply occasions of display, the modern position of the wife and the modern emotions of jealousy are alike unintelligible. Our attitudes toward our children are equally evidences of this same cultural goal. Our children are not individuals whose rights and tastes are casually respected from infancy, as they are in some primitive societies, but special responsibilities, like our possessions, to which we succumb or in which we glory, as the case may be. They are fundamentally extensions of our own egos and give a special opportunity for the display of authority. The pattern is not inherent in the parent-child situation, as we so glibly assume. It is impressed upon the situation by the major drives of our culture, and it is only one of the occasions in which we follow our traditional obsessions" (75).

The conventions of the text

O'Neill restlessly tried different dramatic forms and theatrical conventions to return to the theme of repression and desire. In his play *The Great God Brown* (1925), two different actors wore masks to express different aspects of the same character. In *Strange Interlude* (1926–1927), characters spoke their subtext directly to the audience as "interior monologues." In *Lazarus Laughed* (1925–1926), there is a masked chorus with, according to O'Neill, the "seven general types of character," including the "Self-Tortured" and the "Introspective." In *Desire Under the Elms*, with the rich source material of the Hippolytus story and the intimidating examples of brilliant verse treatments by Euripides and Racine, O'Neill applied the New England dialect he had used earlier in his Pulitzer Prize-winning *Beyond the Horizon* (1920).

The homely language is the equivalent of the bleak physical landscape. The flat tones of the characters are as much a part of the world as the stones of the earth or the animals in the barns. O'Neill's tin ear—a serious problem in other texts (to which his foreign admirers are happily deaf)—contributes to the consistent pattern of the world of the play. According to the aesthetics of our world, O'Neill's lines can seem ludicrous, especially the use of *ay-eh* for "yes," said in flat tones like the *moo* of a cow:

> ABBIE I—I killed him, Eben.
> EBEN (*amazed*) Ye killed him?
> ABBIE (*dully*) Ay-eh . . .

And a few lines later:

> EBEN Not—not that baby!
> ABBIE (*dully*) Ay-eh!

The division between passion and the poverty of passion's expression reinforces the pattern of repressed emotional characters in a repressed world. The effect is to evoke emotion by what is not said and to characterize emotional expression as stingy.

Despite its seeming poverty, the dialect used by O'Neill has rules and its own riches. In the climax of the play, when Eben decides to suffer along with Abbie, she says what is laughably trite:

> ABBIE (*forcing a smile—adoringly*) I hain't beat—s'long's I got ye!

But notice that the dialect forces a line reading. The overly familiar and lovesick "So long as I got YOU" is impossible, since *ye* cannot be extended that way. The emphasis must be placed on *got*: "So long as I GOT ye." This reinforces that, in the world of this play, possession is a much stronger value than love. O'Neill could have written the line as *yew*, a form he uses a few lines before:

EBEN . . . I'd suffer wuss leavin' ye, goin' West, think' o' ye day an' night, being out when yew was in—(*lowering his voice*) 'r bein' alive when yew was
dead.

The forms of language used in any play can be examined for structure. Verse drama,
of course, is written to dramatize the structure of speech. In Racine's 1676 version of
the same story, speech on stage is in the form of twelve-syllable rhyming couplets. The
rule is that a thought ends with the end of a line. When Racine's stepmother, Phèdre,
fails to complete her thought—five times in a row!—it's a signal that she has lost her
mind and can no longer control herself. Here is a description of the celebrated French
actress Rachel (from Chapter 2) performing the role in Russia:

Rachel begins with full voice the tale of her criminal love. Soon the words,
the couplets, as if driven by the thought, begin to run as incredible, barely au-
dible speech. . . . In mid-monologue, Phèdre, giving herself up totally to a
single thought, loses self-consciousness and is almost beside herself. Her lips
tremble, her eyes blaze with a maniacal fire, a gesture becomes insanely ex-
pressive, that ghastly whisper goes on the whole time, and the words run on,
filled with agonizing truth (76).

O'Neill gives his stepmother a wild cry, which set among the *ay-eh*'s, flies free:

ABBIE Don't ye leave me, Eben! Can't ye see it hain't enuf—lovin' ye like a
Maw—can't ye see it's got t'be that an' more—much more—a hundred
times more—fur me t'be happy—fur yew t' be happy?

From these and other speeches we can deduce one more rule: *In the world of this play, to
be happy is desire's defiance of morality.*

The conventions of the production

The physical production and the director's concept also affect the meaning of performances, as anyone doomed to stand onstage trapped in a stupid costume or buried under
a ton of scenery can tell you.

The original production of *Desire Under the Elms* was staged in a cut-away house
designed by Robert Edmond Jones, based on a sketch by O'Neill. This setting had
realms as well as rooms. Upstairs, there were the father's room and the son's room.
The stepmother had the power to see through those walls, just as she had the power
to move from father to son. The kitchen and the parlor were downstairs. Early in the
play, the parlor was established as the dead mother's realm. The stepson brought his
stepmother into the parlor to meet his dead mother, who haunted the place. When
the long-closed parlor window shade was rolled up, and later, when the glass in the
same window was shattered, these were understood by the audience to be the dese-
cration of a tomb.

Other aspects of the production's scenery added meaning. In a play where walls are essential and proper for restraint, protection, defense, and identity—a broken wall and an open gate are significant as a breach in the social order.

> SIMEON The halter's broke—the harness is busted—the fence bars is down— the stone walls air crumblin' an' tumblin'! We'll be kickin' up and tearin' away down the road!
>
> PETER (*drawing a deep breath—oratorically*) Anybody that wants this stinkin' old rock-pile of a farm kin hev it. T'ain't our'n, no sirree!
>
> SIMEON (*takes the gate off its hinges and puts it under his arm*) We harby 'bol- ishes shet gates, an' open gates, an' all gates, by thunder!
>
> PETER We'll take it with us fur luck an' let 'er sail free down some river.

When Simeon and Peter lifted the gate, the pattern of the play was announced again: *Gates will be abolished by the sons of the father who put them there.*

Other aspects of a production can and do contribute to the pattern of the world. Costume in the world of *The Maids* and music in the world of *Yerma* are good examples. Up until the early 1800s, actors portraying Othello on the London stage wore a British general's redcoat, stressing both the role's military rank in the pattern of the play and the virtue of obeying orders. The London actor William Macready (remember how his Macbeth had instigated riots?) wore a turban and pointy shoes as Othello, which set up a pattern of the exotic Orient with its associations of menace and mystery. Ira Aldridge played the same role in what looked like a Greek chiton with a cape, placing his Othello in line with other classical heroes. In the eyes of his European audiences, Aldridge also wore the mask of his skin. So did the black actor Paul Robeson, born ninety-one years after Aldridge, who played Othello to acclaim in London and on Broadway in the twen- tieth century. To the audiences watching Aldridge and Robeson, the sight of a black man among white men would create a different pattern: an Othello strong enough to defy a racist world by loving a white Desdemona, yet weakened by his isolation from the rest of society. In Aldridge's case, such isolation would have been heightened since he alone spoke English onstage while the actors around him spoke another language. This was also the case for Tommaso Salvini, who played Othello in a turban and spoke Italian while American actors performed around him in English.

As you see, casting can affect meaning. Consider the possible implications for a modern American audience if, in a production of *Desire Under the Elms*, the stepmother was played by an African-American woman. In 1850, this would indicate a remarkable strength of will on the part of the father; it might also demonstrate his attitude toward his wife as a possession. Two more rules, then, derived from the conventions of specific productions:

- In the setting of *Desire Under the Elms*, the kitchen is the common area; anyone may come there. The parlor, where the dead are laid out, is the elite area. Only those who respect the dead may enter.

- In the New England world of *Desire Under the Elms*, it is uncommonly rare to be of African descent. An African-American woman cast as Abbie brings to the role the connotations of a freed or runaway slave—or, perhaps more significantly, the rarity in 1850 of an African-American born free.

The Play Will Create Its Own Categories for Rules

Any play will have a unique set of values that configure its pattern. Fertility in *Yerma*, rococo elegance in *The Maids*, and correct speech in Shaw's *Pygmalion* are all issues of importance in their own plays, but unimportant or nonexistent in other plays. In *Desire Under the Elms* there are meaningful categories of birth mother/stepmother, freeman/slave, hard/soft. Other aspects of the production contribute meanings to the play: dance is mean-spirited, the parlor is a haunted tomb, and rock and stone stud the earth and stick in men's hearts.

Notice also that the characters' *names* are part of this pattern. In the New Testament, *Peter* (which means "rock") is the name given by Jesus to the fisherman with the Hebrew name of Simeon. By virtue of their names, O'Neill's Peter and Simeon share the same character, and in more ways than one. O'Neill's Peter and Simeon can be understood as two more lumps of stone on Ephraim Cabot's farm. Ephraim, according to the Old Testament, means "God hath caused me to be fruitful in the land of my affliction."

Let's review the interpretation of the rules for *Desire Under the Elms*:

- The sky and the earth are beautiful. Men are not beautiful; they are manure.
- The savage power of the body is strong. Civilization is weak.
- Wisdom is knowledge that the world is hard. It is ignorant to think there's an easy out.
- It's good to be hard; it's bad to be soft.
- It is skill to squeeze money out of rocks; it is inept to give money away, or let it be stolen.
- It is common to work the soil and to pay attention to traditional values. It is elite to ignore them.
- It is polite to conserve your emotions: to compress them, numb them, control them. It is rude to waste them.
- People survive by doing their chores, by serving a hard master.
- People improve by suffering.
- It is impossible to win. You can only escape, by death or emigration to a new country, in this case California.

For the actors playing Simeon or Peter, the scene where they leave is a departure for Paradise. There is no information given about what subsequently happens to them. In real life, the journey to California was hard. But in *Desire Under the Elms*, the journey is out of the picture, beyond the frame. It's as if Simeon and Peter have died and gone to heaven. In the context of the world of the play, these characters are allowed a happy ending—because they are escaping the hard, tragic life of their father and brother.

One Scene Helps You Interpret Another

Even before the main characters of the play arrive and the plot begins, our analysis of the early scene with Simeon and Peter supplies rules that help define the rest of the text. When later events in the play do occur—the stepmother kills her child, the father discovers his money has been stolen, the stepson decides to accept punishment with his lover—the characters' behavior can be understood more clearly by measuring that behavior in the context of the play, rather than by assigning it arbitrary significance as episode, image, or task. The stepmother kills her son because in the world of this play a child is primarily a possession, and more so, desire is so strong that it subverts even the "natural" love a mother is supposed to feel for her child. The father learns that his life savings have vanished, but the loss does not destroy him; it sets him on to more hard work, which is his survival skill. The stepson accepts punishment because, in this world, life is hard, softness is an illusion.

> EBEN I'd suffer wuss leavin' ye, goin' West, think' o' ye day an' night, being out when yew was in— (*lowering his voice*) 'r bein' alive when yew was dead. (*a pause*) I want t' share with ye, Abbie—prison 'r death 'r hell 'r anythin'! (*he looks into her eyes and forces a trembling smile*) If I'm sharin' with ye, I won't feel lonesome, leastways.
>
> ABBIE (*weakly*) Eben! I won't let ye! I can't let ye!
>
> EBEN (*kissing her—tenderly*) Ye can't he'p yerself. I got ye beat fur once!
>
> ABBIE (*forcing a smile—adoringly*) I hain't beat—s'long's I got ye!

In the world of the play, Abbie and Eben are losers. Cabot, the father, is the one with skill and knowledge to survive. His comment on that last bit of dialogue:

> CABOT Ye make a slick pair o'murderin' turtle doves! Ye'd ought t' be both hung on the same limb an' left thar t'swing in the breeze an' rot—a warnin' t'old fools like me t' b'ar their lonesomeness alone—an' fur young fools like ye t' hobble their lust. . . .

At the end of the same speech, when Cabot realizes he's lost all his money, he says:

> CABOT . . . God's lonesome, hain't He? God's hard an' lonesome!

From this, we can infer another rule of the play: *In the world of this play, people improve by suffering. They may not win or lose except by death.* We may disagree about God in our world, but we cannot argue about it in the world of O'Neill's play. Here, under the elms, Cabot is stingy, ugly, hard, powerful—and wise.

Let's Review Terms

world of the play	the place where the action of the play takes place
rules of the world	what organizes the behavior and the environment
pattern	a more or less consistent configuration of words and action in the play
the ten questions	answering them defines the rules

In the world of this play, what is beautiful and what is ugly?
In the world of this play, what is strong and what is weak?
In the world of this play, what is wisdom and what is ignorance?
In the world of this play, what is skill and what is ineptitude?
In the world of this play, what is common and what is elite?
In the world of this play, what is good and what is evil?
In the world of this play, what is polite and what is not polite?
In the world of this play, how do people survive?
In the world of this play, how do people improve?
In the world of this play, how do people win or lose?

The places to find answers to the ten questions:

- The play itself
- The time and place
- The playwright's system of values
- The form of the play
- The form of the production

The Chart

- **Basic unit.** The given norms of *behavior and form.*
- **The relative theory.** Ruth Benedict's ideas of *cultural anthropology* are a model for a world of the play analysis.
- **Key question.** *What are the values of the play?*

CHAPTER 2

PLAYING BY THE RULES—OR NOT

Learning the Rules

Like Gulliver sailing from one island to another, let's reevaluate how an actor inhabits the world of the play by the measure of a different time and place—the baroque age of seventeenth-century France.

One thing that never changes from age to age is the difficulty of starting a theatrical career. In 1643, in hopes of becoming a professional actor, twenty-one-year-old Jean-Baptiste Poquelin renounced his right to succeed his father as upholsterer to the King. Upholsterer to the King was not a bad job to come into: the furniture-obsessed Louis XIV was next in line. Despite his enthusiasm for the stage, Jean-Baptiste Poquelin's professional beginnings were disastrous. *He acts with his eyebrows*, sniffed a certain Mademoiselle Poisson in her *Memoirs* ("Miss Fish," her name translates to in English) (77). Poquelin spoke too quickly, too harshly. His voice was so strained he was prone to hiccups. The company he formed with the more experienced Béjart family went bankrupt. He was sent to jail. His father paid his debts and bailed him out. Like Stanislavsky, Poquelin eventually changed his name to save his family embarrassment. From then on he was known as Molière (77).

For the next thirteen years, the Paris-born Molière toured the French provinces, mostly in the south. His acting improved through repetition, observation, and hard work—and by contact with another member of the company, the Italian actor Tiberio Fiorelli. Fiorelli was best known for playing the popular commedia dell'arte character Scaramouche with startling physicality. Onstage, Fiorelli could freeze his body in the midst of frantic action and fall silent. Molière was a good pupil of Fiorelli's and learned, among other things, restraint. He even improved his diction, although his rubber face and eyebrows remained irrepressibly mobile.

Nevertheless, the improvements in his craft gained Molière status, and after five years of touring he became the manager of his troupe. In 1658, the company had the opportunity to play a double-bill for the King in a little room at the Louvre. The tragedy they performed was forgettable, but Louis laughed at the farce, written by Molière, entitled *The Doctor in Love* (*Le Docteur amoureux*). *Monsieur*, the King's cross-dressing brother, liked the troupe so much he gave them his patronage.

Molière had fifteen more years to live. During that time he wrote and staged over thirty-two texts: comedies, farces, satires, and interludes for pageants. He had the wit to include his own eccentricities in the characters he wrote for himself—often that of a man blinded to common sense by enthusiasm and subject to various manias for money, religion, status, or a complacent wife.

Although better known to history as a playwright, Molière was nevertheless first and last a performer. In 1673, he was carried off the stage after having had a fit while playing a hypochondriac, a role he wrote to include his unstoppable cough (a malady that had replaced his hiccups). He died a few hours later, before he had time to renounce his profession, as was the custom necessary to receive holy rites. In death, as in life, Molière was bound within the rules of his society. The parish priests refused to bury him until the King intervened.

Playing by the Rules

Molière wrote no books explaining his craft, yet when Louis requested that Molière dramatize a rehearsal, the playwright-actor complied with the play *The Versailles Impromptu* (1663)—in which the playwright depicted himself rehearsing the actors of his company. He criticizes them for not following the ways of other troupes, and in doing so he reveals his own skills by comparison. Other actors paused unnaturally before beautiful passages of verse, from which we can conclude that Molière's actors spoke according to sense, not effect. Other actors were impossibly cast as young people when they were old, from which we can deduce that Molière's company were cast appropriately to type. Other actors ranted and raved in order to show off their voices; Molière's actors were more subtle.

To their contemporaries, Molière's actors were refreshingly unaffected in performance—even when they spoke in twelve-syllable rhymed couplets and acted love scenes facing the audience, not each other. When they played fops and aristocrats, actors of Molière's era took to the stage teetering on high-heeled shoes, corseted at the waist, and topped by powdered wigs. They wore little pads stuck under their tights to make their legs look fashionably plump. For purposes of decorum, they held their arms parallel to the stage floor, so that the lace on their cuffs didn't droop. They placed their feet in ballet-like positions, the legs turned out from the hips, the better to display those lovely calves.

There were people who sat watching these performances who were themselves teetering on heels, corseted, powdered, bewigged, and padded. They took lessons to fence and dance, and considered their own movements to be cultivated and graceful, not affected. Our contemporary manner of movement, devoid of harmony and lace cuffs—on or off a stage—would have seemed barbarous to them.

A world of the play analysis is obviously necessary for actors preparing to perform a text as stylized as Molière's, if only to be able to make sense of the baroque behavior and arcane references. Yet simply copying the flamboyant details and gestures of Molière's period will not create dramatic action for an actor. Analyzing the world of the play involves something other than copying exotic physical styles. This is recognized, by the way, even among the members of Molière's troupe—which endures three hundred years later. Now called the Comédie Française, the troupe proudly retains and passes down even the improvisations of the original performers. But the actors recognize that these tricks are the outer and not the inner substance of their inheritance.

Breaking the Rules

The value of a world of the play analysis for the actor doesn't lie in its ability to reproduce history or imitate reality, but in its ability to create meaning. The words and behavior seen and heard in a play by Molière, as in any other play, are dramatically significant because they establish dramatic actions and human relationships. Hedda Gabler is an *outcast*, Shlink is an *instigator*, and Molière's impostor Tartuffe is a *hypocrite*—despite the style of performance. As long as the words of the play stay as they are, and the dramatic situations they call for are performed, a pattern of relationships will emerge in production. For example, in the 1660s love scenes were sometimes played with both partners facing the audience. Following the guidelines set out in the previous chapter, a world of the play analysis might interpret such a stage convention as a rule: *In the world of this play, the public display of emotion is more important than the emotion itself.* Other scenes, with other displayed emotions, will then be understood within this pattern.

Against the measure of the world of the play, onstage behavior becomes dramatic action when it *disrupts the pattern already established*. For example, let's look at scenes we've already analyzed. When the Professor stumps the Pupil, this event has dramatic significance because it contrasts with the Pupil's quick and ready answers to previous questions. When Yerma defies her husband, it has dramatic significance in light of her previously passionate resignations to God and her husband's will.

Onstage behavior also becomes dramatic action when it represents a *return to the status quo that has been disrupted*—the slaughter of the unstoppably perverse Richard III, the punishment of Abbie and Eben after their desire oversteps New England conventions, or the arrival of the King's messenger who restores justice in *Tartuffe*.

Molière understood about disrupting patterns. He even wrote about it in a petition to the King, in which he defended *Tartuffe* against charges of blasphemy:

> The comic is the outward and visible form that nature's bounty has attached to everything unreasonable, so that we should see, and avoid it. To know the comic we must know the rational, of which it denotes the absence, and we must see wherein the rational consists . . . incongruity is the heart of the comic . . . it follows that all lying, disguise, cheating, dissimulation, all outward show different from the reality, all contradiction in fact between actions that proceed from a single source, all this is in essence comic (78).

A world of the play analysis identifies the dynamic between what Molière calls the rational and the unreasonable. Bewigged or not, the play's patterns will assign certain onstage events significance as dramatic action, just as a melody assigns value to certain notes. Actors preparing and rehearsing a role in any play should understand the meaning of their behavior and dialogue within those patterns. Guided by this understanding, which is the product of rehearsal and private preparation, episodes will be reinterpreted, tasks will lose and gain priorities, and images will form new and varied constellations as sense memory or fantasy.

The Rules of the Strange and the Familiar

Preparation for a role in a stylized play like *Tartuffe* inevitably suggests the need for a world of the play analysis, if only for the technical reasons of articulating the verse and making sense of the lines. As we've noticed in *Macbeth* and *Richard III*, the language of a verse play is significant in its form and content. As retorts and rejoinders, the exchange of words is essential to the action. Even in translation, it is important that the audience understands every spoken syllable. A vocal technique different from the one you would use for O'Neill's nuanced *ay-eh*s is required to deliver rhymed couplets or blank verse. Performing a play like *Tartuffe* often also requires studying and practicing stylized gestures. If performing in period dress, you will need to learn how to move in the costumes without tripping or ripping—one more specialized skill, like vocal technique, required to act the text and inhabit the world of the play.

Yet, each text of Molière's plays configures its patterns differently: the mania for religion is not the same as the mania for money or for a quiet spouse. Although they come from the same sources in time and space, each of Molière's plays has a distinctly different world, just as individuals from the same era had distinctly different personalities. There should be no blanket "Molière style" with which to smother creativity among the actors or the differences between texts.

By the way, too much concern for period detail can divert a performer's attention from the search for the more significant pattern of the whole text. It is the pattern of *behavior and words*, not exotic details, that a world of the play analysis tries to identify and apply in rehearsals and performance. Once again, Ruth Benedict's insights in the field of anthropology—that anthropologists struck with the oddness of foreign customs lose sight of the cultural patterns that make such exotica understandable—can point the way to improve an actor's process.

Like social anthropologists turning their attention from the unsmiling Dobu Islanders (remember them?) to modern society, let's now examine ways to develop the world of the play by rehearsing a scene—not from *Tartuffe*, but from Neil Simon's *The Odd Couple* (1965) (79). A familiar and relatively modern comedy can better illustrate, with less distractions than a baroque period piece, how any play can be better rehearsed and performed by applying world of the play analysis.

A comedy like *The Odd Couple* calls for actors to master the technique of getting an audience to laugh, but a comic technique is simply a collection of arbitrary tricks if applied to a play without respect for the meaning of the text, even a play as seemingly obvious in its meaning as *The Odd Couple*. Neil Simon's text isn't just a collection of jokes. The play is about something, and world of the play analysis helps to identify what that subject matter is. To dramatize the subject matter, *The Odd Couple* displays a pattern of behavior and dialogue as strong and distinctive as O'Neill's *Desire Under the Elms*. World of the play analysis can help you identify that pattern, and then playfully use that knowledge to support other techniques and approaches to acting—including the ones that get laughs.

Analyzing the World of *The Odd Couple*

Begin your preparation by yourself

World of the play analysis can begin as you read the play alone at home, and perhaps after you've look at related background material suggested by the setting of the text and the circumstances of its writing. If you have no copy of the script, you'll have to begin preparation after you've heard the script read aloud. Your interpretation will change as you rehearse, of course. Still, preparation you do by yourself will help you begin rehearsals with some idea—even if mistaken—of what you are saying to other people. This way you can make sure you don't resemble Gilda Radner's deaf television commentator who got herself worked up defending violins on television, until she realized the topic was *violence* on television. Never mind. A good way to begin is by answering the ten questions listed in the previous chapter.

This chapter reviews practical ways to apply a world of the play analysis to rehearsals. In order to proceed to those skills, let's agree on the premise of an interpretation. You may come up with different answers to the ten questions, but you can apply them in the same ways. It doesn't matter which interpretation you choose, as long as you can demonstrate its validity by speaking the words of the play—since those are the words you share with an audience.

Neil Simon wrote *The Odd Couple* between 1964 and 1965. The story concerns two men, estranged from their wives, who share an apartment in New York City. Felix is compulsively neat, Oscar is a slob. The new bachelor roommates recreate the circumstances of their marriages. Their individual habits, which drove their wives to separate from them in the first place, now drive the guys to distraction and to a new separation—from each other. Productions of the play have been very successful. The original production of *The Odd Couple* ran on Broadway for years, and in 1968 Neil Simon adapted his script into an equally popular movie.

In order to begin with a premise, then, here are answers to the ten questions about the world of *The Odd Couple*:

- *In the world of this play, what is good and what is bad?* The answer to this question is an excellent example of how values in the play as a whole redefine the values of any single character. Being neat is good for Felix. Being a slob is good for Oscar. Within the play, neither one extreme nor the other is good. Being too neat is bad, being too casual is bad. What is good is the middle, reasonability. What is bad is extreme.
- *What is beautiful and what is ugly?* Friendship and sharing are beautiful. Selfishness is ugly. The love between two friends is what is most beautiful in this play.

- *What is ignorance and what is wisdom?* Ignorance in this play is sticking to your guns, wisdom is knowing when to give in. Wisdom is graceful submission and apology.
- *What is polite and what is not polite?* The etiquette of the play is that of the middle class of the mid-1960s. Good manners are soft and gentle; bad manners are loud, outspoken, and gruff. Contained is polite, messy is rude. Felix is polite. Oscar is rude. But polite is not always good, nor is rude always bad. Common sense overrides manners in this world.

The play takes place in Felix's apartment, where the men's buddies gather once a week to play poker. These poker-playing pals are the real barometer of reasonability throughout the play. Even the "regular guys" think Oscar's lack of housekeeping is extreme. Before Felix tidied it up, Oscar's refrigerator had been broken for two weeks. One of the poker players claims to have seen milk standing in there—and it wasn't even in the bottle.

- *How do people survive?* By compromise. This is the secret for the play's success with middle-class audiences; it establishes the middle road as the road to achievement. That doesn't make it a bad play. It doesn't make it a good one, either. It might explain its popularity.
- *How do people improve?* By reaching the golden mean, by getting along with their neighbors.
- *How do people win or lose?* They don't. This is a play where the characters interact but don't change their relative positions, and it is for that reason that it could be so skillfully adapted into a television series. The series ran from 1970–1975, 114 half-hour treatments of the same characters' relationship—none of them written by Neil Simon (who thought the idea of an *Odd Couple* television series odd).

Onstage or on screen, Felix and Oscar don't win or lose. They go on being extreme, and then compromising for the sake of love between friends—until the next chance for selfishness arises. That is why the situation is funny: whenever the friends break the rules, eventually they are forgiven and return to the bosom of the partnership. No matter what the characters do, they end up the same way, with the possibility of renewed happiness.

After effortlessly completing the first two acts of this play, Simon had trouble writing the third and final act. Perhaps the reason is that the pattern of the action is repetitive. As it reads now, at the play's end Felix is about to return to his wife and Oscar is beginning to reconcile with his wife over the phone. But in our hearts we know it won't happen. Two television series and a film sequel later, it still hasn't happened. Back to our questions:

- *In the world of this play, what is strong?* What is common to all men—love wins out over the individual. The needs of the group are stronger than the desires of the individual.
- *What is common and what is elite?* Married men are elite, single men are common. Single women are elite, married women are common. In *The Odd*

Couple, we meet relatively few elite people. The class distinctions in the play are few, and for a reason: the unspoken assumption is that we're all basically middle-class. This reflects the mid-1960s American worldview.

- *What is the ultimate skill?* Bargaining. Knowing how to negotiate. Giving enough away, but still having your own.

So a pattern is established that structures the behavior of the play: *Selfishness gives way to love between friends. The highest good is friendship and compromise.*

The Odd Couple is set in the era in which it was written: New York in 1965. The text includes jokey references to New York neighborhoods, which implies that its audience shared an understanding that Rockaway was far away (it's a beach, several miles from the center of Manhattan); and that the Upper West Side faced the coastline of New Jersey. The year 1965 was a "middle year," a period of American history when the country stood tall, confident in itself. John Kennedy had been gone long enough for Lyndon Johnson to be measured in his own right as President of the United States—reelected the year before by a landslide majority. Counterculture challenges to that majority—like the Black Power movement, the Sexual Revolution, and hippies—were thunder on the horizon, if perceived at all. The small concerns of middle-class life (too neat or too messy?) could take on dramatic metaphor without touching on politics. Part of the pleasure of the play for contemporary audiences is that it offers an oasis of such petty concerns.

On a personal level, Neil Simon was just under forty years of age when he wrote *The Odd Couple*, and he was still with his first wife. He had his second big success on Broadway two years before with *Barefoot in the Park*, and the optimistic and happy *Odd Couple* is influenced by that perspective. Simon's later plays—after a few flops and a few more wives—are neither as sunny nor as funny (deliberately). They reveal introspection gained from experience.

Now, you may disagree with the above interpretation. You may offer other ideas: that the play is a version of Neil Simon's two aspects, *the nerd* and *the adventurer*—described by the playwright in the introduction to the collection of his first plays. You may disagree that compromise is the highest good in *The Odd Couple*; you may say that integrity is the highest good, and point to examples in the text. You may demonstrate that love wins out in the end. You may comb through Neil Simon's many generous interviews in which he has answered questions about *The Odd Couple* to prove that the playwright contradicts every answer given to the above ten questions. It doesn't matter. Choose what you want, and let's begin to rehearse the play applying whatever set of rules you've defined for the world of the play. For now, accept these answers to the ten questions as a premise from which to proceed.

Apply the rules to tasks, episodes, and images

Let's look at a scene from the second act, when Felix has arranged a date for himself and Oscar with the Pigeon Sisters, two British ladies who live in the same building. These comic siblings announce their own meaning: not Pidgeon like Walter, but pigeon like coo-coo pigeons. When Oscar goes in to get drinks for the coo-coo sisters, Felix is left to entertain them.

> FELIX *turns and faces the girls. He crosses to a chair and sits. He crosses his legs nonchalantly. But he is ill at ease and he crosses them again. He is becoming aware of the silence and he can no longer get away with just smiling.*

FELIX Er, Oscar tells me you're sisters.

CECILY Yes. That's right. (*she looks at* GWENDOLYN)

FELIX From England.

GWENDOLYN Yes. That's right. (*she looks at* CECILY)

FELIX I see. (*Silence. Then, his little joke*) We're not brothers.

CECILY Yes, we know.

FELIX Although I am a brother. I have a brother who's a doctor. He lives in Buffalo. That's upstate in New York.

GWENDOLYN (*taking a cigarette from her purse*) Yes, we know.

FELIX You know my brother?

GWENDOLYN No. We know that Buffalo is upstate in New York.

FELIX Oh! (*he gets up, takes a cigarette lighter from the side table and moves to light* GWENDOLYN'S *cigarette*)

CECILY We've been there! Have you?

FELIX No! Is it nice?

GWENDOLYN Lovely.

> FELIX *closes the lighter on* GWENDOLYN'S *cigarette and turns to go back to his chair, taking the cigarette, now caught in the lighter, with him. He notices the cigarette and hastily gives it back to* GWENDOLYN, *stopping to light it once again. He puts the lighter back on the table and sits down nervously. There is a pause.*

Felix's *task* is *to put the girls at ease*. His *obstacles* are his own clumsiness and physical awkwardness. A reference to the world of the play orients Felix's tasks more precisely. Within the pattern of the play, Felix's desires are invariably connected to and balanced against Oscar's. Here, the balance works like this: Felix would prefer to stay home and clean; Oscar wants some excitement and maybe a little fling. Oscar is divorced and available for other women; Felix is separated, not yet divorced, and very much attached to his family. Felix's task in entertaining the coo-coo sisters is to keep them in a good mood until Oscar returns with their drinks. An additional obstacle to Felix's task is the ladies' interest in Felix, which flusters him.

World of the play analysis also identifies *opportunities* to fulfill tasks. According to the manners of 1965 middle-class America, pious girls neither smoke nor drink. If the aim is to find willing partners for Oscar, the opportunities in the scene are identified by the fact that the ladies are smoking and waiting for alcohol to be served. These girls are *swingers*, out for a good time.

> FELIX Isn't that interesting? How long have you been in the United States of America?
> CECILY Almost four years now.
> FELIX (*nods*) Uh huh. Just visiting?
> GWENDOLYN (*looks at* CECILY) No! We live here.
> FELIX And you work here too, do you?
> CECILY Yes. We're secretaries for Slenderama.
> GWENDOLYN You know. The health club.
> CECILY People bring us their bodies and we do wonderful things with them.
> GWENDOLYN Actually, if you're interested, we can get you ten percent off.
> CECILY Off the price, not off your body.
> FELIX Yes, I see. (*He laughs. They all laugh. Suddenly he shouts towards the kitchen*) Oscar, where's the drinks?
> OSCAR (*offstage*) Coming! Coming!

World of the play analysis will also redefine *episodes* and the value of *transactions*. Felix and the girls trade social gestures. The world of this play defines this as the exchange of polite, not very intrusive, personal information. Felix offers clichés, which entail little: "I have a brother in Buffalo." The Pigeon sisters offer innuendoes, which entail a good time, if not a good deal: "People bring us their bodies and we do wonderful things with them." Felix will not pick up on the girls' innuendoes or successfully light Gwendolyn's cigarette because he will not trade his politeness for what they are offering. The actors playing the sisters need to understand this in order for the episode to make sense. The exchange of the cigarette is an incomplete *gest*, because it is a failed exchange.*

> CECILY What field of endeavor are you engaged in?
> FELIX I write the news for CBS.
> CECILY Oh! Fascinating!
> GWENDOLYN Where do you get your ideas from?

---

*World of the play analysis helps clarify episodes we've identified in previous chapters. The episodes that accumulate during *In the Jungle of Cities* are all better understood within the context of the play. If we agree that the pattern of life in Brecht's vision of Chicago is a pitiless contest for survival, the episode's caption, PEACEFUL MAN DRAWN INTO VIOLENT STRUGGLE TO SURVIVE, can be refined by a world of the play analysis to THE VICIOUS SNAKE ATTACKS THE SLEEPING MONGOOSE. A similar reorganization of *Richard III* takes place when you understand that the episodes in which the hunchback appears all undermine the natural order of who is King of England—until the final episode where the natural order rises up and obliterates Richard. One of the captions we've already arrived at for Act I, scene ii, KILLER HUNCHBACK PITCHES WOO TO VICTIM'S WIDOW, could be further refined to THE IMPOSTER KING STEALS THE WIFE OF A HERO.

FELIX (*he looks at her as though she's a Martian*) From the news.

GWENDOLYN Oh, yes, of course. Silly me . . .

CECILY Maybe you can mention Gwen and I in one of your news reports.

FELIX Well, if you do something spectacular, maybe I will.

CECILY Oh, we've done spectacular things but I don't think we'd want it spread all over the telly, do you, Gwen?

They both laugh.

The *images* of a text are major components of the world of the play. British accents might evoke *stuffy formality* to you. In *The Odd Couple*, British means *swingers*, not crumpets and tea. The names of the girls wink at this change from prim to permissive: Gwendolyn and Cecily are the names of the proper young ladies in Oscar Wilde's *The Importance of Being Earnest*. In 1965, to a Broadway audience savvy enough to laugh at jokes about Rockaway, London meant Mod London and Carnaby Street, the source of raised hemlines, lowered morals, and libertine behavior. America may have been standing tall in 1965, but London was swinging. So, if you're playing one of the Pigeon sisters, you'd better find something that works for you to swing before you get yourself buttoned up in the image of a prim British maiden.

Notice how the characters form a composition

The two Pigeon Sisters are virtually identical giggling twits—or are they?

CECILY Oh, we've done spectacular things but I don't think we'd want it spread all over the telly, do you, Gwen?

They both laugh.

FELIX (*he laughs too, then cries out almost for help*) Oscar!

OSCAR (*offstage*) Yeah, yeah!

FELIX (*to the girls*) It's such a large apartment, sometimes you have to shout.

GWENDOLYN Just you two baches lives here?

FELIX Baches? Oh, bachelors! We're not bachelors. We're divorced. That is, Oscar's divorced. I'm *getting* divorced.

CECILY Oh, small world. We've cut the dinghy loose too, as they say.

GWENDOLYN Well, you couldn't have a *better* matched foursome, could you?

FELIX (*smiles weakly*) No, I suppose not.

GWENDOLYN Although technically I'm a widow. I was divorcing my husband, but he died before the final papers came through.

FELIX Oh, I'm awfully sorry. (*sighs*) It's a terrible thing, isn't it? Divorce.

GWENDOLYN It can be—if you haven't got the right solicitor.

CECILY That's true. Sometimes they can drag it out for months. I was lucky. Snip, cut and I was free.

FELIX I mean it's terrible what it can do to people. After all, what is divorce? It's taking two happy people and tearing their lives completely apart. It's inhuman, don't you think so?

CECILY Yes, it can be an awful bother.

GWENDOLYN But of course, that's all water under the bridge now, eh? Er, I'm terribly sorry, but I think I've forgotten your name.

FELIX Felix.

GWENDOLYN Oh, yes. Felix.

CECILY Like the cat.

FELIX *takes his wallet from his jacket pocket.*

The characters in a play acquire meaning by *comparison* with each other. Oscar is the messy one, Felix the neat one. If Gwendolyn is the taller sister, Cecily becomes the shorter (or is it the other way around?) The New Yorkers are the locals, the standard; the British girls are the outsiders, exotic, and available. The audience understands these differences and identifies characters by comparing role to role, as if the roles formed a **composition**.

The Odd Couple has been adapted for a number of situations, but regardless of the changes in circumstances, the dynamic composition of the characters remained the same. In Portugal, there was a television series, not a dubbed version of the American show, but one with a Portuguese setting and characters. In 1982–1983, an American television version was set among middle-class African-Americans. In 1985, Neil Simon himself wrote a new stage version with female characters in the leading roles named Olive and Florence; the Pigeon sisters converted into the Costazuela Brothers from Barcelona, Spain. Again, in all of these variations the essential composition of characters remained the same: divorced people of the same sex live together, one neat, one messy. The scene we are examining here appears in all of them. A date is arranged for a possible good time, which Felix/Florence ruins.

In other plays we've examined, the contrast in characters sharpens their identity. In *Desire Under the Elms*, Simeon and Peter are the older, duller sons who escape their father's hard rule. Eben, by way of contrast, is the younger, brighter son who challenges his father. In *Hedda Gabler*, the composition of characters is essential to establish that Hedda is a misfit in the world she inhabits. Ibsen mentions that Hedda's old schoolmate, Thea, has healthy, thick blonde hair—the better to point up Hedda's thinning, dark hair and general ill health.

The relationships between the roles can make much more of a setting for the play than any walls. Think of the composition of *The Maids*: the mistress-who-is-to-be-killed, the elder-maid-who-arranges-the-killing, the younger-maid-who-does-the-killing. In *Yerma*, the happy women with children who surround Yerma contrast with the barren Yerma's misery.

As for the two Pigeon sisters, the playwright offers some clues for differences: one had a happy marriage that turned sour, the other had a marriage that was always bad. But more importantly, if you are one of the actors playing these roles, your individual character will be established by how you play against your "sibling": *I'm the slow one, she's the fast. I'm the blonde, she's tastefully gray.* Or, the two of you can agree that there are no differences and you're both the same—like the Rockettes. If the two sisters are played as amusingly identical, that too is based on rules. You'll both be blonde or both be gray, and certainly you'll speak with the same British accent.

Playing (and rehearsing) by the rules

Just as the play will suggest new categories for value, it will suggest new ways to rehearse. If you agree that the Pigeon sisters resemble each other, then you will need to rehearse that resemblance. In *The Maids*, the maids imitate Madame. The actresses who play these three roles will have to rehearse the gestures, tones, and other traits they mean to share as Madame.

Other plays will suggest certain skills that you'll need to master in rehearsal. In *The Lesson*, the speed at which the characters speak is a crucial dynamic that indicates the Pupil's ability to dazzle and the Professor's ability to baffle. Rehearsals could very easily take place with a metronome marking an accelerating beat or music underscoring the scene with ever-quickening tempi. This is the director's business to suggest, but even if the director doesn't do anything so creative, *you* can—on your own. You could also practice certain things, like speaking more rapidly, and apply them to rehearsal.

The skills required of one play, of course, are not those required of another. The precision of a Vermont accent for *Desire Under the Elms* will not really help in the Upper West Side milieu of *The Odd Couple*—but the quick delivery of vaudevillian comedians would be well worth studying, copying, and stealing.

The rules of conduct for *The Odd Couple* are that of *social politeness*, which might be gleaned from an etiquette guide from the period. During polite conversation, when a subject is brought up, it should be followed up by the listener, however inanely:

> FELIX I have a brother who's a doctor. He lives in Buffalo. That's upstate in New York.
> GWENDOLYN Yes, we know.
> FELIX You know my brother?
> GWENDOLYN No. We know that Buffalo is upstate in New York.

Polite conversationalists find points of common interest:

> FELIX We're divorced. That is, Oscar's divorced. I'm getting divorced.
> CECILY Oh, small world. We've cut the dinghy loose too, as they say.

Sadness and negativity should be unmentioned, or turned positive:

FELIX It's inhuman, don't you think so?

CECILY Yes, it can be an awful bother.

GWENDOLYN But of course, that's all water under the bridge now, eh?

There are other, unspoken rules: when you're with someone you're interested in, you don't talk about your ex-wife. Felix takes out pictures of his children, and praises his ex-wife to the skies. The girls gamely follow along:

FELIX (*taking pictures out of his wallet*) That's her, Frances.

GWENDOLYN (*looking at the picture*) Oh, she's pretty. Isn't she pretty, Cecily?

CECILY Oh, yes. Pretty. A pretty girl. Very pretty.

FELIX (*takes the picture back*) Thank you. (*shows them another snapshot*) Isn't this nice?

GWENDOLYN (*looks*) There's no one in the picture.

FELIX I know. It's a picture of our living room. We had a beautiful apartment.

GWENDOLYN Oh, yes. Pretty. Very pretty.

CECILY Those are lovely lamps.

FELIX Thank you! (*takes the picture*) We bought them in Mexico on our honeymoon. (*he looks at the picture again*) I used to love to come home at night. (*he's beginning to break*) That was my whole life. My wife, my kids—and my apartment. (*he breaks down and sobs*)

CECILY Does she have the lamps now too?

FELIX (*nods*) I gave her everything. It'll never be like that again. Never! I— I— (*he turns his head away*) I'm sorry. (*He takes out a handkerchief and dabs his eyes.* GWENDOLYN *and* CECILY *look at each other with compassion*) Please forgive me. I didn't mean to get emotional. (*trying to pull himself together, he picks up a bowl from the side table and offers it to the girls*) Would you like some potato chips?

CECILY *takes the bowl.*

It wouldn't be a bad idea to read a 1965 Emily Post *Guide to Good Manners* and try to apply its rules to the day's rehearsal.

Other plays have harsher, more life-crushing rules of etiquette. Lorca identified Yerma's central problem as the inflexible, life-denying institution of marriage. Practice holding your spine rigidly in emulation of the properly brought-up Spanish villager (who carries water from the well in a bucket balanced on her head), and you will gain an appropriately austere posture for Yerma. The rules binding Hedda Gabler, we know, drive her to kill herself. In rehearsing any of these scenes, it is very helpful to understand how the social environment restrains the action, or permits it to fly free—like Simeon and Peter once they lift up the gate.

Breaking the rules is dramatic action

Once the audience is accustomed to the rules of the pattern, they will feel that any behavior or words that break the rules are dramatic actions. In *The Odd Couple* that can mean losing your temper; in *Macbeth* it can mean speaking with twelve beats to a ten-syllable line.

When rule-breaking is punished, the pattern of the play can be called *tragic*. In classical tragedies like *Oedipus the King*, rule-breaking is followed by the obliteration of rule-breaking characters as individuals; when the pattern resumes, the rule-breakers are folded back into the group. Often definitions of tragedy apply the rules of offstage morality, or philosophy, which ends up excluding, say, Arthur Miller's *Death of a Salesman* as tragic, because the story does not conform to an idea of ancient Greek responsibility. True, the salesman of the title, Willie Loman, doesn't break the rules of his world; Miller's play is not about that. What the play is about is the way the system of Willie's life flouts the rules of nature, which overwhelm Willie, and everyone around him, as he grows old. In the same way, Richard III's evil ways and Macbeth's ambivalent wrongs are overwhelmed when the natural order of the world—the rightful succession of King—rises up and reasserts itself.

When rule-breaking is forgiven, the pattern of the play can be called *comic*. Often, a comic plot is a series of errors that lead to the correct answer. The characters are secretly obeying the pattern they seem to flout. In classic comedies, very often the character's rule-breaking attacks that world's definition of the role the character is supposed to play. Respectable fathers turn fools, servants talk back to the masters they are meant to obey, pious leaders prove hypocritical, heroes prove cowardly, women take on men's roles. By the end of the play, the behavior that challenged the pattern is forgiven, or, in some cases, leads to a rearrangement of the pattern. Sometimes the pattern of the play is revealed to be different from what was previously thought, and the hero who seemed to be so ridiculous was secretly on the right track to revealing a new aspect of the world.

A performer should understand the pattern of the play enough to say whether it's comic or tragic. Interpretations such as Hedda Gabler's heroism will be supported by the framework of the play. Interpretations that try to emphasize the tragic loneliness of the two expatriate Pigeon Sisters will be undermined by the pattern of the play. In a comedy like *The Odd Couple*, breaking the rules is funny, and then forgiven.

GWENDOLYN You mustn't be ashamed. I think it's a rare quality in a man to be able to cry.

FELIX (*puts a hand over his eyes*) Please. Let's not talk about it.

CECILY I think it's sweet. Terribly, terribly sweet. (*she takes a potato chip*)

FELIX You're just making it worse.

GWENDOLYN (*teary-eyed*) It's so refreshing to hear a man speak so highly of the woman he's divorcing! Oh, dear. (*she takes out her handkerchief*) Now you've got me thinking about poor Sydney.

CECILY Oh, Gwen. Please don't. (*she puts the bowl down*)

GWENDOLYN It was a good marriage at first. Everyone said so. Didn't they, Cecily? Not like you and George.

CECILY (*the past returns as she comforts* GWENDOLYN) That's right. George and I were never happy. Not for one single, solitary day.

> *She remembers her unhappiness, grabs her handkerchief and dabs her eyes. All three are now sitting with handkerchiefs at their eyes.*

As an actor, it is important you break the rules without calling attention to yourself or winking at the audience that you know better. Usually, the character breaks the rules without thought to the consequences:

FELIX Isn't this ridiculous?

GWENDOLYN I don't know what brought this on. I was feeling so good a few minutes ago.

CECILY I haven't cried since I was fourteen.

FELIX Just let it pour out. It'll make you feel much better. I always do.

GWENDOLYN Oh, dear; oh, dear; oh, dear.

> *All three sit sobbing into their handkerchiefs. Suddenly* OSCAR *bursts happily into the room with a tray full of drinks. He is all smiles.*

OSCAR (*like a corny M.C.*) Is ev-rybuddy happy?

The episode is organized to recognize that the rule is being broken. The *gest* here is everybody sobbing into their handkerchiefs, which is translated into the world of the play as FELIX RUINS OSCAR'S CHANCE TO MEET NEW WOMEN. Certainly this is how *Oscar* understands the event, and for once, the audience is meant to understand it in the same way.

Satisfy the audience by following the rules

An audience is satisfied when the pattern of the play is completed, in the same way that they can be satisfied by the completion of a melody while listening to music. In order to achieve this connection to your audience, you can use your understanding of the pattern to shape the through-line of your tasks, organize the progression of your transactions, or channel the transformation of your images.

There is the possibility for the audience to feel deep satisfaction at the end of *The Maids*, for example, because the servants who have been rehearsing the murder of Madame finally realize their dream of killing someone—even if it's Claire in the place of Madame. There is a similar satisfaction possible at the end of *Richard III* when the usurping monster is finally stopped. As a performer, your shaping the pattern of actions gives the audience an understanding of the significance of events: Hedda's suicide, the Pupil's death, Anne's seduction. Although the rules of a world are often announced, the consequence of rule-breaking is more often demonstrated with behavior and reactions. In a comedy, there is a particular pleasure in seeing how, through a chain of errors, the rule-breaking character ends up following the rules after all:

> OSCAR (*like a corny M.C.*) Is ev-rybuddy happy? (*then he sees the maudlin scene.* FELIX *and the girls quickly try to pull themselves together*) What the hell happened?
>
> FELIX Nothing! Nothing! (*he quickly puts his handkerchief away*)
>
> OSCAR What do you mean, nothing? I'm gone three minutes and I walk into a funeral parlor. What did you say to them?
>
> FELIX I didn't say anything. Don't start in again, Oscar.
>
> OSCAR I can't leave you alone for five seconds. Well, if you really want to cry, go inside and look at your London broil.
>
> FELIX (*he rushes madly into the kitchen*) Oh, my gosh! Why didn't you call me? I told you to call me.
>
> OSCAR (*giving a drink to* CECILY) I'm sorry, girls. I forgot to warn you about Felix. He's a walking soap opera.
>
> GWENDOLYN I think he's the dearest thing I ever met.
>
> CECILY (*taking the glass*) He's so sensitive. So fragile. I just want to bundle him up in my arms and take care of him.
>
> OSCAR (*holds out* GWENDOLYN'S *drink. At this, he puts it back down on the tray and takes a swallow from his own drink*) Well, I think when he comes out of that kitchen you may have to.

The pleasure in this is that Felix, by doing everything wrong as a host, has outshone Oscar, who has been doing everything right.

By yourself again, look at all the incidents at once

When the incidents of the play are looked at all at once, a pattern will emerge. This technique was identified as **spatial analysis** by the Shakespeare critic G. Wilson Knight. It can be used by a performer to review and reorganize what has taken place in rehearsals. All the scenes in *The Maids* can be seen as variations of the same murderous episode; all the tasks of *The Lesson* can be seen as variations of the same obsessive supertask; all the descriptions of *Desire Under the Elms* can be seen as variations of the same stony imagery. All episodes in *The Odd Couple* can be seen as variations on the act of finding a way to give in, to meld the extremes. Any task of Felix's is balanced against a task of Oscar's. The images of the characters are complementary; they bring out each other by contrast. By recognizing what is the same throughout those plays, you can begin to create for your performance what is distinct, because what is distinct is a *variation* within the pattern. Bring your understanding to rehearsals as a way to further refine your choices.

Let's Review Terms

dramatic action	a significant breach in the rules
tragic pattern	when rule-breaking is punished
comic pattern	when rule-breaking is forgiven
composition of characters	characters are defined by comparison to other characters
spatial analysis	to look at all the events of the play as if they happened at once, in order to define a repeated pattern

Notebook:
Analyzing the World of the Play

Following the rules:
Felix is there is to keep
the girls interested in Oscar—
Breaking the rules:
—but not in himself!

FELIX *turns and faces the girls. He crosses to a chair and sits. He crosses his legs nonchalantly. But he is ill at ease and he crosses them again. He is becoming aware of the silence and he can no longer get away with just smiling.*

crosses his legs: Legs crossed,
at the ankles, not like a woman or an
effeminate man. Important to register
that he is attracted to the women,
not oblivious to them (and attempt
to seem *strong*)

just smiling: To *survive* in this
situation, but not to improve
or to win

FELIX Er, Oscar tells me you're sisters.

CECILY Yes. That's right. *(she looks at* GWENDOLYN*)*

FELIX From England.

GWENDOLYN Yes. That's right. *(she looks at* CECILY*)*

FELIX I see. *(Silence. Then, his little joke)* We're not brothers.

CECILY Yes, we know.

you're sisters: The safest thing for him
to say (he knows this already) *(Skill)*

Silence: The worst thing that can
happen, during conversation *(Bad!)*
his little joke: It's *smart* to think
of something amusing to say
to put them at ease.
(*Skill* in finding a subject
that is noncommittal)

FELIX Although I am a brother. I have a brother who's a doctor. He lives in Buffalo. That's upstate in New York.

GWENDOLYN *(taking a cigarette from her purse)* Yes, we know.

FELIX You know my brother?

GWENDOLYN No. We know that Buffalo is upstate in New York.

FELIX Oh! *(he gets up, takes a cigarette lighter from the side table and moves to light* GWENDOLYN'S *cigarette)*

I have a brother:
Filling the gap *(Polite)*

Gwendolyn smokes: A loose girl!
Oscar will like that (single and
available, a *rare bird*, this Pigeon)

Buffalo: Not very interesting *(Inept)*

CECILY We've been there! Have you?

FELIX No! Is it nice?

GWENDOLYN Lovely.

> FELIX *closes the lighter on* GWENDOLYN'S *cigarette and turns to go back to his chair, taking the cigarette, now caught in the lighter, with him. He notices the cigarette and hastily gives it back to* GWENDOLYN, *stopping to light it once again. He puts the lighter back on the table and sits down nervously. There is a pause.*

FELIX Isn't that interesting? How long have you been in the United States of America?

closes the lighter on her cigarette: Felix's proximity to the girls arouses and startles him. He doesn't want to be aroused, so he doesn't look too closely into Gwendolyn's eyes, which is why he makes the mistakes. *(Weak, polite, inept)*

Not really listening, although it's important to keep the appearance that he is deeply interested. Most important to keep a look of interest on his face. *(Polite)*

CECILY Almost <u>four years</u> now.

FELIX *(nods)* Uh huh. <u>Just visiting?</u>

GWENDOLYN *(looks at* CECILY) No! We live here.

FELIX You work here too, do you?

CECILY Yes. We're secretaries for <u>Slenderama.</u>

GWENDOLYN You know. The health club.

CECILY People <u>bring us their bodies</u> and we do wonderful things with them.

GWENDOLYN Actually, if you're interested, we can get you ten percent off.

CECILY Off the price, not off your body.

FELIX Yes, I see.

four years/just visiting: It's *inept* to reveal he's not paying attention to what they say.

Slenderama: The name is trendy, so are they—beauty! And Oscar will like this! *(Good!)*
bring us their bodies: Not picking up the innuendo, not hearing it *(Ignorant)*

> *He laughs. They all laugh. Suddenly he shouts towards the kitchen.*

FELIX Oscar, where's the drink?

OSCAR *(offstage)* Coming! Coming!

He laughs: The laugh of the girls clues him into the risqué nature of the joke *(Knowing)*

Suddenly he shouts: The delayed reaction to the sexual offer, *losing his own cool* (by shouting) suddenly *wise to what's going on.* Afraid that he has compromised himself, Felix calls for help. *(Surviving,* just barely—with the help of his friend: the highest good)

Practical Tips for Working

Let the artwork of a period shape your thinking

Being familiar with art from the periods in which a play is set or created will shape your ideas as a performer. Remember that the forms of art in any era have a range as distinct as personalities and social classes. Picture the differences between seventeenth-century baroque painting praised at court and the French folk art that flourished during the same time—each practiced by a very different group of artists and appreciated by a very different public.

Listen to the music. The music of a period is as telling as a heartbeat. American jazz groups touring to Berlin inspired the steady pounding drums of Brecht's city-jungle; Viennese elegance drifting through the Scandinavian out-lands provided the lilting waltz of Hedda Gabler's dancing days (and Henrik Ibsen's, too). Not every character will enjoy the same music. In *The Odd Couple*, the radio dial probably swings between Felix's classical station and Oscar's sports reports before it settles on what they both can agree on—Gershwin, perhaps. Definitely not rock and roll, since connotations of sexual freedom are outside of this world. Not country and western, either. New Jersey is as far west as this world reaches. If you can feel what an intrusion country and western music would be in this Upper West Side apartment, you already have a sense of the borders of the world of *The Odd Couple*—as well as that world's lack of a frontier.

Learn the moves. From Japan to France, the national theaters that specialize in evoking long-gone worldviews conduct rehearsals that are often accompanied by period music. Sometimes, actors learn dance steps and movements even before they learn their roles or the lines of the play. If theater tells the story of human relationships, social dances are the poems of human relationships.

Learning to dance a minuet is an excellent introduction to the court of Louis XIV, where proper display was the highest of virtues. Like all court dances, the minuet was performed by a group that faced the King. The formation seen by Louis was more important than the individual steps or the expression of an individual dancer. The men's legs were turned out from the hips to make a good impression; a woman displayed her rank and position by what hung between her legs—literally: stitched on the wide front of her dress was her family's coat of arms. In life, as onstage, flirtations between dancers took place with partners looking straight ahead, not at each other.

Other physical activities shape a worldview. The hard work of farming a poor soil instills the patience and resignation designated as superior values in the world of *Desire Under the Elms*. For plays set or written in England during the early 1700s—when gentlemen studied fencing—an actor could appropriately use dueling terms such as *attack*, *counter-thrust*, *retreat*, and *parry* to evaluate the way characters exchanged their cutting remarks.

Pay attention to what you (and other characters) are wearing. Clothing, shoes, and underwear disclose the conventions of any time and place, including a play's. Big hips, little waists, white skins, dark skins, big feet, little feet—all have had different worth in different places and times. In performance, corsets, push-up bras, padded shoulders, and pointy shoes all mold the body, for better or worse, according to changes in the rules of beauty. Shoes, from cowboy boots to satin slippers, are literally the "under-standing" of a character.

While he was writing *Yerma*, Lorca was also at work on a play called *Doña Rosita*, the story of a fifteen-year-old girl (Rosita), affianced in 1900, who remains faithful to the lover who abandoned her. In 1925, at the age of forty,* Rosita accepts that her fiancé will never return and that she has become a spinster. The demise of Rosita's world, a pattern organized around the central value of hope, can be understood by following the parade of hats worn by the ladies who visit Rosita over the three acts of the play. The hats of 1900, when Rosita is fifteen, look like luxuriant flower gardens. The hats of the second act, when Rosita is thirty, are still flamboyant, but are set on a more structured frame. The last set of hats, from 1925, are felt flapper caps worn close to the head—reduced in line in the same way the characters are reduced in all the other circumstances of their lives.

Look around you. The spaces in which people live will necessarily shape their view of the world, and their behavior. The gilded salons of Molière's settings induced an aristocratic hauteur that would be deflated by the squat dark furniture chosen by Auntie Juju to fill Hedda Gabler's salon. Neil Simon writes in his memoirs that the idea for *The Odd Couple* took shape when he could picture the apartment in which the play was set—complete with its dying goldfish and bachelor-pad mess. With this flash of inspiration came the comic possibilities of finicky Felix's housecleaning disrupting Oscar's squalor.

Look at artwork. The visual arts lend a period its shape and forms. Experience of the visual arts will do the same for you, widening your vocabulary of gestures and poses so that they may become specific to the world of the play. The chunky woodcuts of Shakespeare's day parallel the crude vigor of representation in Elizabeth's England, onstage and off. Rigaud's famous portrait of Louis XIV—note the fashionable stance of the King's thigh toward the viewer—was stamped on Molière's actors and audiences as the proper way to display themselves. After the First World War, Georg Grosz and Brecht revealed to weary Berliners that they were not alone in feeling like animals. More than that, Grosz's savage etchings and Brecht's plays gave their public a vocabulary with which to express their intuitions.

Read something other than the play. Your grasp of the conventions of a world created by a play can be strengthened by reading other plays, poetry, fiction, or contemporary newspapers (if there were any) from the time and places the play was written or set. A good trick is to look at the popular works of the period that are now considered to be dated. You can apply the Spanish theory that says the second-rate literature of a culture reveals more about that culture than the first-rate literature (which is, by its excellence, not bound by the specifics of its time and place). If you're preparing to play Jean Genet's maids, better read *True Detective* magazines; Solange and Claire say they do.

The non-dramatic texts written by playwrights are particularly helpful to under-

---

*The dates for *Doña Rosita*'s setting are confusing. The published text gives as a subtitle: *A Tale of 1900 Grenada.*

stand the worldview of their plays. Chekhov's short stories are a wonderful introduction to his compassion and irony. Brecht's poetry is very beautiful, and offers an insight into his heart. Shakespeare was working on his sonnets while he put sardonic sweet nothings into the mouth of the hunchback Richard III.

What to do without a full script

World of the play analysis considers the play as a whole, but this is impossible when actors are handed their lines and their cues—and nothing more. This was and is still common practice in Eastern Europe. At the first rehearsal, The Leader—the director or author—reads the entire script out loud while the cast listens intently. Then the actors receive their sides (pages with only their scenes on them) and get no more chances to learn about the rest of the play until late in rehearsals, when the whole play is rehearsed in sequence. The claim was and is that this saves paper. The other claim is that an ensemble needs to be sensitive to each other, and over time will have learned to play off each other. Maybe. Maybe it has more to do with the idea that only the Leader can know the whole plan; everyone else learns to do their own job and not worry about the purpose.

For whatever excuse, all too often film scripts give the actors only the words of the scenes they are in, and sometimes only the cues. Keeping actors ignorant reinforces the authority and intelligence of the director, casting director, and producer. It's sad but true: working in a film, you will often not have the materials to prepare yourself to enter the world of the performance. In a play, if you don't have a full script, you can derive clues from your costume, the settings, and especially from what the other actors are doing. Simeon and Peter's scene in *Desire Under the Elms* sets the rules for the world of the play, even before the plot begins and the main characters of the story enter.

Work within the world of the production

The physical aspects of a production—lighting, scenery, costumes, the architecture of the theater—assign meaning to your acting, and you should learn to play within the measure of those circumstances. You'll especially want to understand how the physical production makes you stand out—or disappear. There is a play by Samuel Beckett, *Happy Days* (1961), in which a woman sits up to her waist in a pile of sand. Although she's immobile, she is alive; she still has her memories and counts them among her blessings. After an intermission the audience returns to find the same woman now buried *further* up to her neck in sand and still counting her blessings. "Another happy day!" she chirps (80). Her clichés, which would be trite in the world of the audience, are, by the measure of the sand, the forceful weapons of a hero bravely fighting off resignation and death.

The specifics of the production, even those that can't be seen, can also organize *images* you use, even the most personal images of yourself and others. In the film version of Edward Albee's *Who's Afraid of Virginia Woolf* (1966), Elizabeth Taylor, after years of being treated as a beautiful object to be photographed, delivered the performance of her lifetime because she had a chance to use her self-knowledge of her own image—and the public's response to that image—within the world of the production. That world was established when Taylor and her real-life husband Richard Burton were cast as husband and wife in the film. The Burtons' reputation as a decadent royal pair, given to tempestuous battles and impetuous love, provided Taylor (and her public) a powerful Rosetta Stone for translating what it meant in the world of a small New England college campus to be a college president's daughter who drunkenly argues in public with her husband, demeaning him for not being the head of his own department.

Perform with the logic of absurdity

Samuel Beckett, the author of *Happy Days*, is the most important of a group of playwrights, who, in the years immediately after the Second World War, created a body of work set in surreal worlds divorced from identification with specific times and places. Perhaps this is a response to the nationalism of the two World Wars and the Cold War after: when people have nothing in common, perhaps the one thing they do have in common is what is strange to all of them.

Beckett, who was Irish, wrote his plays in France and in French, but translated them into English himself. He is usually considered to be an English writer. Eugene Ionesco, the Romanian author of *The Lesson*, wrote in French, and conceived his most famous play, *The Bald Soprano* (1950) (81), from the dialogue found in an English-language primer. This is the first line of that play, spoken after the clock strikes seventeen:

> MRS. SMITH There, it's nine o'clock. We've drunk the soup, and eaten the fish and chips, and the English salad. The children have drunk English water. We've eaten well this evening. That's because we live in the suburbs of London and because our name is Smith.

This is not a realistic England, and it isn't meant to be.

In 1951, the British critic Martin Esslin categorized these plays as the *theater of the absurd*. The word *absurd* does not justify erratic and arbitrary onstage behavior. The rules within such plays are absurdly different from the rules among the audience, but nevertheless they are rules for the behavior of the characters. We've already examined a scene from Ionesco's *The Lesson* for tasks and obstacles, and discussed the logical outcome of absurdly unquestioning obedience.

The texts of Samuel Beckett's plays create dramatic landscapes with rules consistent enough to have resulted in an adjective, *Beckettian*, that describes the similarities of the blasted wastelands in which the plays are set and the behavior that takes place in those landscapes. Grim humor often serves as a survival tactic. Discussing the Beckettian view seen out the window of a featureless room in Beckett's *Endgame* (1957) (82), two characters exchange the following lines:

> HAMM Is it night already then?
> CLOV *(looking)* Gray. *(louder)* Gray! *(louder)* GRRAY! *(whispers in his ear)*

HAMM Did I hear you say gray?
CLOV Light black.

Beckett resisted translating his landscape to recognizable settings. In 1984, when the American director Joanna Akalitis tried to place *Endgame* in a New York City subway station, the playwright protested and asked his lawyers to close the production.

Other playwrights have created alternative worlds meant to lie adjacent to recognizable settings, populated by the clichés of a national character. Harold Pinter in England, Luigi Pirandello in Italy, Jean Genet in France, Peter Handke in Germany, Slawomir Mrozek in Poland, Edward Albee and Sam Shepard in America—all have created texts that evoke worlds in which the façades of a benign national identity are revealed as fronts for a sinister parallel world. Actors performing in these plays are meant to act in such a way as to convince the audience that the parallel world behind the façade is *also* a norm and a reality, not just a disruption or an illusion.

The illusion of reality—onstage and in films

Sometimes a play, like the reflection in a mirror, gives the audience the impression of a real world. Remember Hamlet's instructions to the actors he hires?

> . . . the purpose of playing, whose end, both at the first and now, was and is, to hold, as 'twere, the mirror up to nature . . .
>
> *Hamlet, Act III, scene ii*

Follow Shakespeare's image through and think carefully about what mirror-makers do: they put silver on the back of glass, or polish steel to brilliance, or use some other technique to create a reflection of reality. They don't hold up an empty frame. They don't polish *glass*, or paint *steel* from behind. They use the techniques specific to the medium in which they work.

Techniques for creating a convincing illusion vary from play to play, just as they do from mirror to mirror. The realistic world of *The Odd Couple* has every one of its characters unrealistically deliver comic zingers with deadpan regularity. The realistic world of *Hedda Gabler* requires unrealistic eloquence of speech. The realistic world of *Desire Under the Elms* restricts the actor to an unrealistically limited vocabulary. Actors performing in these realistic plays must identify the specific skill—comic timing, fine speaking, or plain speaking with a hint of repressed passion—that is necessary to make their unnatural behavior seem believable within the frame of the individual play.

Creating these illusions of reality for an actor requires submersion in the world of the play, which, at its best, will result in the transformation of an actor's accent and physique into elements of the production. This work is familiar from film. It is fascinating to watch the work of Robert De Niro throughout his long career. For *Bang the Drum Slowly* (1973), De Niro traveled south to learn that region's way of life and speech; for *Taxi Driver* (1976), he worked twelve-hour shifts in a cab. The next year, for *New*

York New York, he learned to play the saxophone. The year after that, to prepare for *The Deer Hunter* (1978), he spent weeks among Ohio Valley steelworkers. Most famously, for his performance two years later in *Raging Bull* (discussed in Chapter 6), De Niro worked out for months in a boxing ring and gained fifty pounds to play heavyweight fighter Jake La Motta at different stages in his life, from lean and mean contender to bloated ex-champ.

Within the rules of the world of *Raging Bull* (much of which takes place among Italian immigrants), blondes are elite. La Motta marries a blonde. A quarreling wife is common; La Motta gives his wife plenty of reasons to quarrel with him. Winning is beautiful, losing is ugly. Ignorance is thinking you can become champion without the help of gangsters. Wisdom—something La Motta never seems to acquire—is knowing how to get along with the powers that be. Sexual jealousy is a sickness; sexual desire, healthy. Within the rules of the boxing ring, flab is not just ugly, it's *bad*. A trim belly is good; a fast right hook is better. To swing out is inept, to wait for the time to land a blow is skill. Getting hit in the head is all in a day's work.

Speaking in an interview of how his research and preparation shapes his performances, De Niro has said:

> There was a scene in *Raging Bull*—one of the scenes where I went back to the corner after knocking somebody down. I was doing too much because I didn't know what to do, and it was the first fight scene that we shot. I was jumping up and down a little too much. When you see actual fighters, they do that. But they also just wait in the corner. It's like anything else. In the beginning you learn the rules, and then you realize that the rules are there to use or not to use and that there are millions of different ways of doing something (83).

Include the audience

Though the audience doesn't necessarily share the rules that structure the onstage world, they should appreciate, if not always understand, the *significance* given in the world of the play to behavior and action. In order to shape the audience's perception, onstage reactions become as important as actions to establish these values.

For example, Molière's world can be reproduced onstage with some degree of accuracy. But no research can resurrect the original audience for whom red heels were the height of fashion and Louis XIV a living presence to be feared. How an actor portraying an onstage courtier *reacts* to the presence of the King, however, will convey to a modern audience Louis's life and death powers.

An odd problem arises when the audience thinks they understand what's going on, but do not. Neil Simon has noted that his plays do better in other countries of the world than in England—because in other countries the plays are translated idiomatically. In England they are performed in the original language, of course, but the British audience does not value or react to American idiom in the same way as an American audience. As the British comedian Benny Hill used to say: "What is this thing *called*, Love?"

When the audience can be led to share the rules of a long-gone period, texts that seem impossibly dated can spring to life within the *rules of the era*. A good example of how this can succeed is the story of Sarah Bernhardt's 1903 revival of Jean Racine's play *Esther*, written in 1689.

In 1689, Racine had been retired from the stage for twelve years. His retreat was prompted by the religious powers at the French court who had persuaded Louis to shun the playwright. Racine's sympathetic portrayal of a sexually eager woman in *Phèdre* was denounced as a bad influence on the morals of the country. At the suggestion of the King's pious consort, Madame de Maintenon, Racine took up a subject from the Bible. He chose the story of Esther rescuing her people from the wicked plans of an evil courtier, and wrote a play on this theme to be performed at a convent girls' school—Madame de Maintenon's favorite charity.

When Bernhardt revived the play in 1903, she reproduced the conventions of the original production. Actresses played all the roles, including the men, as if they were school girls. What brought the world of the play into focus was the presence in the audience of actors portraying the aristocrats, Louis XIV among them, who had condescended to view the original production (84).*

Esther is not a great play, but its world of simple, heartfelt truth triumphing over evil-minded politics was understood by and moved its audiences—in Racine's day and in Bernhardt's. Sarah herself played the Persian King of the production as an awkward adolescent girl with an obviously fake beard. Her voice broke and her beard slipped, but she did her best. This performance is a good example of how to create a convincing illusion by working within the conventions of a world. In 1903, when she was playing this adolescent "King," Bernhardt was fifty-nine.

The Chart

- **Unifying image.** The world of the play acts as a *frame* to organize behavior onstage so that it becomes significant form.
- **Dramatic action.** Dramatic action is a *breach in the rules of the world*.
- **The intended reaction of the audience.** The aim of the performer is to *transport the sensibilities of the audience* to the onstage world, so that they feel, if not always understand, the disruptions and returns to the pattern of the play.
- **The illusion of character.** The illusion of character is understood in *the context of the world*; a role is characterized as part of a *composition* of other characters and the environment.
- **Suitable playwrights.** World of the play analysis is particularly useful when preparing to work on texts written by playwrights whose worldview is distant from our own in time and place: *Molière, Oscar Wilde*, the Restoration playwrights; also, authors who create alternative and artificial worlds: *Beckett*,

---

*The description of the production in Cornelia Otis Skinner's book *Madame Sarah* is well worth reading—although she does get the date of *Esther* wrong.

Ionesco, all verse plays, including *Shakespeare*; and playwrights who seem to be creating a world that they repeatedly visit: *Tennessee Williams, Genet, Pinter, Strindberg,* and *O'Neill.*

Is There a Right Way to Do It?

Is Bernhardt's reproduction of *Esther* the only way to stage that play? Was Samuel Beckett right—morally right, aesthetically right—to want to close down a production of his *Endgame* set in a New York subway station? Is there a *correct* world for some plays, a world inextricably bound to an appropriate style intended by the playwright or the age in which the play was first presented?

The answers to these questions have to do with property, not just propriety. Beckett's lawyers insisted that he owned and controlled the world of the play just as much as he owned the legal rights to its text. "National" theaters worldwide make similar claims to their nation's literature as their rightful heritage, and regard foreign interpreters as trespassers who lack respect, authenticity, and shame. In various theaters and schools from Paris to Tokyo, actors who enter the profession take on a lifelong submission to the discipline of preserving and passing on theatrical traditions. Once they dictate the rules laid down by their models, these schools reward continuity, not originality, and demand single-minded devotion to a closed system. In India it's a flexed foot, in France it's a hand parallel to the stage, among the Maoris it's a wagging tongue, in Japan it's a hidden thumb. These all have meanings within their separate styles. Very often, after years of repetition, the shape of an actor's body changes: hips spread, fingers fold back, toes curl—on their own.

Such sincere dedication demands respect, just as sincere religious beliefs demand respect, even if one doesn't share those beliefs. Traditional theaters cater to audiences trained to appreciate the nuances of their limited vocabularies. Sometimes a play needs more distance from its original style to make its worldview felt by an audience with a different orientation. That different point of view can be an advantage. A Buddhist parable points out that, although they are very close to the eyebrows, the eyes cannot see the eyebrows; only another pair of eyes has the necessary distance.

A living playwright is certainly entitled to prevent the meaning of his words from being perverted, if only out of respect. Yet, if the script is open to only one interpretation—the playwright's—it probably won't survive its author's death, if it lasts that long. Of course, there are undeniable close affinities with the style of a production and the world of the play. Yet even a "national" style interpreting a "classic" text changes from era to era, just as the images of nations change. Stanislavsky's interpretations of Chekhov altered when Russia came under Communist rule and aesthetics, even though the texts stayed the same and the style remained realistic.

The script evokes the world of the play, but only when the text intersects with the shifting points of view of living actors who transmute words into dramatic action. That is the subject of the next chapter: *the dramatic action of a shifting point of view.*

www.ingramcontent.com/pod-product-compliance
Lightning Source LLC
LaVergne TN
LVHW081321060426
835509LV00015B/1628